"*Irreverent Prayers* will  .o
struggle, especially whe 1-
forting prayers' anythi ıd
through the psalter and o-
tions there, these prayers may give voice to allow you to
speak your struggles to God."

—SCOTT GUNN,
executive director of Forward Movement

"Equal parts cheeky and vulnerable, *Irreverent Prayers* offers a refreshing vision of honest engagement with God in the face of significant illness and pain. Written by and for the 'seriously sick,' this book is a vital resource for everyone exactly because it's animated by first-hand experiences."

—BETHANY MCKINNEY FOX,
author of *Disability and the Way of Jesus*

"Here is a book of prayers for the sick like none I have ever seen, written bluntly but tenderly, speaking aloud the confusion, rage, and loneliness—and even loss of faith—that can be brought on by the brutality of serious illness and hospitalization. Felicetti and Vincent-Alexander know all too well the valley of the shadow of death from their own experience and offer us their honest witness and courageous words as a bridge for anyone longing to express to God (and perhaps also other people) what this depth of pain and suffering is like, and how on earth to pray about it when a loving God seems powerless to help."

—HEIDI HAVERKAMP, author of *Holy Solitude*

"This is the book I will reach for when I am in pain. This is the book I will gift to those in pain. *Irreverent Prayers* offers real, holy, and healing prayers."

—TERI OTT,
editor and publisher of *The Presbyterian Outlook*

"The experience of life-threatening illness is an isolating one in a world that teaches that through hard work and a positive attitude, perfect health is your reward. In this book of prayers, Samantha and Elizabeth knock down the silos that keep us quiet about the reality of being human. Their faithful, sometimes funny, always sincere messages to God reveal that while vulnerability is our lot, it can be the force that brings us closer together to one another and to God. This book is a gift."

—MEGAN L. CASTELLAN,
Canon to the Ordinary, Diocese of Central New York

"If the prayers that Elizabeth Felicetti and Samantha Vincent-Alexander have to offer from the vulnerable space of serious illness are irreverent, I don't want to be reverent. Honest, raw, and real is how I imagine God hopes we speak to her, and the words of this prayer book are exactly that, giving form—occasionally edged in wry humor—to the varied emotions associated with being seriously sick. An invaluable tool for anyone experiencing illness, either for themselves or as a pastoral caregiver."

—MEGHAN MURPHY-GILL,
author of *The Sacred Life of Bread*

IRREVERENT PRAYERS

TALKING TO GOD WHEN YOU'RE SERIOUSLY SICK

Elizabeth Felicetti
Samantha Vincent-Alexander

WILLIAM B. EERDMANS PUBLISHING COMPANY
GRAND RAPIDS, MICHIGAN

Wm. B. Eerdmans Publishing Co.
4035 Park East Court SE, Grand Rapids, Michigan 49546
www.eerdmans.com

Book design by Lydia Hall

Printed in the United States of America

30 29 28 27 26 25 24   1 2 3 4 5 6 7

ISBN 978-0-8028-8263-9

Library of Congress Cataloging-in-Publication Data

A catalog record for this book is available from the Library of
Congress.

CONTENTS

INTRODUCTION

"How did you pray?" one of us, Samantha, asked the other, Elizabeth. "When you were in a place like this, how did you pray?"

It was a chilly January night, and Elizabeth had been surprised to see Samantha calling from the ICU in another Virginia city two hours away. Elizabeth's recent time in the ICU flooded her senses, especially the memory of how hard it had been to talk after being intubated for two lung surgeries. Samantha had a potentially deadly infection and was reaching out for prayer advice.

We are both experienced Episcopal priests who lead parishes as rectors. But, despite being a supposed spiritual leader, Elizabeth had found prayer elusive during her earlier stint in the ICU, except for one night: the second night, when she finally capitulated to the nurses and accepted oxycodone, which she had avoided until then for fear of addiction. Breathing was agony with a chest tube. She felt like someone had stabbed her, just missing her heart but leaving a spear lodged inside. That night with the oxycodone, breathing in "Lord Jesus Christ, Son of God" and breathing out "Have mercy on me, a sinner," she had finally been able to fall asleep. Until they woke her up at midnight to make her take Tylenol, which didn't touch the pain.

"The Jesus Prayer?" she suggested. "You know, the one that goes 'Lord Jesus Christ'—"

"I tried that," Samantha cut her off.

"The psalms?" Elizabeth offered next, suspecting that, as a fellow priest, Samantha had already tried that too. Jesus's own prayer book gives voice to feelings of anger and betrayal and abandonment.

Samantha admitted that while she had always loved praying the psalms in the past, she couldn't bring herself to read them now, partly because sleep deprivation made reading difficult and partly because she was afraid that the one thing that had always brought her comfort in the past would do nothing to allay her current anxiety.

Elizabeth hadn't been praying the psalms lately either. The Episcopal Morning Prayer service regularly cycles through the psalms, but Elizabeth had stopped praying a Morning Prayer app back before she was sick and now found her personal prayers most effective—after she had finally returned to church some eight months after surgery, radiation, and chemotherapy—when walking her church's outdoor labyrinth.

But walking a labyrinth wasn't an option right then for Samantha because the infection was in her leg, so she was confined to the ICU bed. So we talked about Tylenol. Samantha also was being awakened at midnight to take the pills. "I think Tylenol has a deal with hospitals," she said.

"And I think they are only allowed to administer it at midnight," Elizabeth replied.

Samantha had almost died. How could this close friend, ten years younger than Elizabeth and with a five-year-old son, be close to death? Elizabeth was the one who had battled lung and breast cancer just over a year before, who now had respites between scans every three months to see if the cancer had come back. Elizabeth remembered how Samantha had comforted her when she'd been deathly ill, texting her in the hospital, instead of calling on the phone, because talking hurt too much; sending her a beautiful meditation calling her a woman of valor; driving two hours to see her in August in the height of the first summer of the pandemic when Elizabeth was undergoing chemo; sitting outside on the deck in the sweltering heat so that they wouldn't share air inside. Those expressions of friendship meant more than prayer, yet both of us are Episcopal priests.

During the Reformation, Anglicans wrote a prayer book instead of a statement of belief. Anglicans pray what they believe. As priests in this tradition, we needed prayers that worked.

"None of the prayers in the prayer book helped me," Elizabeth finally told Samantha. "I am sorry." She felt like she had blown a sacred opportunity. Here she was, the person—the priest—whom Samantha had reached out to, but she didn't have an answer. She felt like she had failed her friend.

Samantha's battle with MRSA (Methicillin-resistant Staphylococcus aureus) led to three surgeries and a second hospitalization before she was sent home on disability with a bulky wound vac. In early March, Elizabeth texted her, "I thought you would appreciate my prayer this morning: 'God, I need to stay healthy because my husband shouldn't have to deal with that bullshit.' Seems like a prayer that should be published somewhere, lol."

Samantha texted back, "We should write a book full of irreverent prayers."

"We could call our book 'Prayers of Irreverent Lament by Two Sick Priests.' Amen! Because when the book you need doesn't exist, you write it with your BFF."

"Dear God: We don't care that you can draw out a leviathan with a fishhook—your response to Job sucks. You can do better."

And it was morning, and it was evening, the first day this book of irreverent prayers was born. We struggled a bit with the word "irreverent." We certainly don't mean unbiblical. We find the prayers in this book solidly biblical. Reverence, however, can be linked to fear. Our parishioners and many Christians are afraid to express their emotions to God. But God took on flesh so that through Jesus God experienced the emotions that we feel.

When the priest Zechariah was told by an angel that he and his wife, Elizabeth, would have a son, John the Baptist, he doubted, and then was unable to speak for months. After the birth he was able to speak again, and when he prophesied he spoke about serving God without fear. That's what we want to do: pray honestly, without fear of God's response to our prayers.

We hope that others seeking prayer when ill can reach for this book when other prayers seem too pious and all they want to do is scream, except they can't because it would hurt too much. We would love it if we could become a blessing to others. When friends call to ask, "When you were in a place like this, how did you pray?" we'd like to provide a pile of reverent and irreverent words that will remind them that they aren't alone.

ONE SICK STORY:
BREASTS AND BREATH

ELIZABETH

On the second day of Christmas, during a painful biopsy on my left breast, I realized that I wasn't fully on board with the incarnation. The Gospel on the first Sunday in Christmas is John's prologue: "the Word became flesh and lived among us." I've long believed this is one of the most beautiful doctrines of the church: God becoming flesh and living among us. God becoming one of us, with a body.

As an Episcopal priest, I preached about God becoming flesh and living among us, but I didn't want my parishioners to know I have flesh; specifically, breasts. Clergy wear long flowing robes over our clothes so parishioners won't focus on our bodies. The only thing harder to contemplate than telling my congregation that I might have cancer was telling them it was *breast* cancer. When God became flesh and lived among us, God didn't have breasts.

I'm not the only female pastor who doesn't want my congregation to think about my body. My friend Samantha has a rule that parishioners can't ever see her in a swimsuit. But Samantha thinks I take this to extremes, since I went years and years without even owning a swimsuit. My husband, Gary, and I belong to a gym with a pool and a hot tub that I won't use. What if a random parishioner comes by? Or really, anyone. I don't want anyone to see me in a swimsuit. The Bible doesn't say what Jesus wore to his baptism, but I imagine him wading into the river in a robe. He became flesh and lived among us, but he wore a robe day and night, until Roman soldiers stripped him and hung him on a cross. Finally, I found a bathing suit that looks like a shirt and shorts, but I still won't wear it at the gym.

I don't even want people to see me in a skirt. I have a closet full of adorable skirts: striped, polka dot, pencil. When I buy them, usually with Samantha, she asks, "Are you actually going to wear this one?" I almost never do, and when I do, for Easter or a biannual bishop visitation, my parishioners comment that I rarely wear skirts, and I remember how when I was a lector at a small church in Chuckatuck, Virginia, a woman told me in an icy drawl that her husband loved it when I read because he enjoyed looking at my legs. The skirts look lovely in my closet.

Do not worry about your body, what you will wear, Jesus said. To me, that sounds like a man. Women are judged by what we wear. I doubt this was different in Jesus's day.

I didn't wear a skirt to the biopsy. The tech pointed to a dingy bathrobe on a stark chair next to a desk surrounded by monitors. On the other side of the room lurked something that looked like a dentist chair facing a mammogram machine. After I put on the robe, which was nothing like the robes I wear on Sundays, the tech said, "I need to ask you these questions. What are we doing today?"

When people address me using first-person plural, I want to punch them. *We* weren't doing anything. *They* were going to stick needles in me.

"Biopsy," I replied, hoping my tone sounded withering, not terrified.

"Actually two biopsies," she corrected, then explained that I would be "compressed" in the scary chair the entire time. She said it shouldn't take more than an hour.

She marked my breast with an ink pen. When a stranger touches my breast, I don't think about God being like me. God became flesh, but not a woman. Jesus did not have breasts, judged for their size and firmness. Jesus looks pretty muscular in most depictions of him on the cross, but imagine if it was a woman hanging there topless. How big would her breasts be? Would they be firm breasts that had never nursed? Jesus said that the days are coming when some will say blessed are the breasts that never nursed, but since my breasts never nursed, I am at higher risk for breast cancer.

When I moved to the chair and said something about dentists' chairs, she winced. "We don't use that word here," she whispered. "People are afraid of the dentist." I like my dentist. The doctor and the nurse came in. The nurse said she was my "hand-holder." I don't need someone to hold my hand at the dentist.

I knew the biopsy—biopsies—would involve needles, but I didn't know I would be "compressed" the whole time. "Compressed" meant I had to slightly arch my back so that my entire breast was painfully pinned between two heavy cool clear plates, which were slowly brought together so that my sensitive breast was smashed lower, lower, lower, the skin of my chest pulled tighter and tighter, my nipple thrust further and further to the front of the machine. I bit the area below my lower lip until I tasted blood. "You won't feel the needles," the tech said.

Before they stuck the needle in they photographed my flattened breast several times, repositioning and frowning.

As the doctor, tech, and nurse took more photos, they kept telling me to lean back. "Further." "Further."

I could barely feel the big needle going in. Perhaps if I could have felt it, I would have thought about Jesus being pierced. About Mary hearing that her own soul would be pierced. But whatever numbed my breast and prevented piercing pain could not disguise that it was smashed.

When they were finally finished, my blood stained the dingy robe. I was swaying when they released me from the machine. "Are you okay?" the tech kept asking.

I finally snapped, "Of course not. That hurt."

We returned for the biopsy results on New Year's Eve. I was sure I did not have cancer, because the nurse who had been my designated hand-holder smiled at me in the waiting room. Then we were in the office, and the doctor was frowning and saying, "the calcifications were harmless, but the other spot of concern contains a cancerous tumor." She kept talking, but I didn't hear anything else.

Gary asked questions and nodded at certain points and looked smart and handsome while the nurse handed me a tissue. I would have skipped a mammogram that year, convinced that they were unnecessary screening procedures that lead to false positives, and only went because he nagged me. If I had not gone and the cancer had progressed and I had died, he would have been even bossier with his next wife. She would have been slim and blonde and athletic. She would have always gotten her mammograms on time, although she would be barely mammogram age when they got married. She would have loved eating salmon, would have gone hunting with him, and could have field-dressed a deer herself. She would have had an amiable ex and a teenage daughter, and they would all spend holidays together. Everyone would say, *So glad he found someone. Elizabeth would have liked her*. But really, I would have known her blonde highlights were fake. She could probably do math, too. Maybe she would have been an accountant, and in tax season her roots would show because she wouldn't have time to touch up her blonde highlights. Fortunately, tax season and deer season are not at the same time. I couldn't hear anything they were saying but just watched Gary's face.

They didn't have a trash can in the room. The nurse offered to take my tissue as we left, but I declined because that was disgusting. When I was a chaplain intern in a hospital, we were taught "If it's wet and not yours, don't touch it." Nurses have to touch other people's wet messes all the time. Chaplains just hold their hands and pray. Both involve touch. Flesh. Incarnation. But chaplains get to be cleaner.

I followed Gary to my car, and even though I had driven to the hospital, I got into the passenger seat. Gary told me I needed to call our insurance company to ensure that the surgeon to whom they had referred me was in network. We argued about this as he turned left from the right-turn lane leaving the hospital, the only indication that my diagnosis had affected him. I pointed out his error as cars honked but he insisted that he had *not* been in the right-turn lane. I asked why he wouldn't call the insurance company his damn self, seeing how his wife had cancer, and he told me, gently, that by doing it myself I would gain some control. "You need some control," he said.

Pressing numbers to reach an insurance person while hearing again and again that I should use their website, I thought, *this is my life now*. I would spend the rest of my life on the phone with insurance companies. No, with *this* insurance company, because no one else would ever offer me insurance again because I had cancer. I was no longer a healthy person.

I had to get my husband's social security number because, even though I am the rector of a parish, to the insurance company I would only be the military member's dependent. I would have to finally memorize his social security number after twenty-three years of marriage because I would have to give it again and again. I had to ask the woman on the phone to repeat things because I couldn't understand what she was saying. She spoke in a bored monotone. This was what she did all day: talk to people about their insurance. Rather than becoming frustrated, I needed to be grateful that I had insurance. I should have felt privileged. I did not.

After finally confirming that the surgeon was in network, I was about to hang up when she said, "ma'am?"

I was a ma'am now because I had cancer, so must be old. Being addressed as "miss" had always annoyed me, but now I did not like "ma'am."

She was waiting for a response. "Yes?" I said, clipped. I'm skilled at sounding chilly.

"I am so sorry about your diagnosis," she said. "But you are going to be fine. My mom and my aunt both had this, and they are fine now. You will be fine, too."

My mouth fell open. I was not expecting kindness.

The next day, New Year's Day, my friend Shirley took me to lunch. Shirley is also the rector of a parish and also had breast cancer. I told her how this whole situation happening during the Christmas season had me ruminating on the doctrine of the incarnation. Christ becoming one of us, with a body.

Shirley said, "Notice that Jesus didn't come as a woman. Why didn't he come as a woman? I'll tell you why: periods and breasts."

"That's a really good point," I said.

She added, "Also notice that he didn't live long enough to have prostate issues like other men."

I reflected on God becoming one of us but male, dying violently before experiencing the indignities of disease and old age. Some sneer that old age is a luxury. I wondered whether I would feel that way soon.

It was still the season of Christmas, and the proper preface for the eucharistic prayer that weekend would include "Jesus Christ . . . was made perfect man of the flesh of the Virgin Mary his mother." I wondered if when I prayed the words again I would long for a less perfect man, one who had experienced disease and blemishes. If now that I had cancer, I would long for God to become, rather than a perfect man, an imperfect woman.

I worried later that my musings about God and the incarnation led to my lung cancer. My second cancer diagnosis was three months after the first, on Holy Week Monday at my dining room table because of the COVID-19 pandemic. Since the shutdown I had thought about all the people whose diagnosis experience would have been so different from my breast cancer diagnosis, unable to sit in a small office with a doctor and a nurse and whatever person they brought. I had envisioned such poor people alone in the office, not at a table in their home with their doctor's face an inch tall on their phone screen.

"We will treat it aggressively," the pulmonologist's tiny head said. "Surgery!" I was lucky. Surgery wasn't always an option with lung cancer.

"I hate to say it, but the breast cancer probably saved your life," said the oncologist's tiny head later. "They wouldn't have found it if it weren't for the radiation scans. You don't have any risk factors." She meant that I was a nonsmoker. I later learned that the biggest risk factor for having lung cancer is having lungs.

Surgery meant an open thoracotomy removing the upper half of my left lung. The Internet said a three-to-five-inch scar, which I told the cardiothoracic surgeon after I ended up with a seven-inch scar. He laughed and showed me that his hands would not fit in a smaller scar. The first surgery, deemed an emergency so able to take place in April 2020, led to a second emergency surgery a few hours later because I bled too much. I named my chest tube "the Spear" because it felt like I had been stabbed with a spear that missed my heart but remained lodged right next to it. While I tried to breathe with the Spear, I thought of the spear in Jesus. The tube connected to a piece of plastic collecting fluid from my body that I had to carry like a suitcase whenever I made my way out of the hospital bed, and I thought about how blood and water had come out when Jesus was stabbed in the side with a spear. I thought of mixing water with wine for the Eucharist, which I could not have because of the pandemic, because churches were shut down along with everything else.

Fearing addiction, I avoided opioid painkillers until the end of the second day, when I overheard other nurses telling mine that if I didn't take them I would never be able to get out of bed. That night, oxycodone coursing through my veins, I prayed the Jesus Prayer—"Lord Jesus Christ, Son of God, have mercy on me, a sinner"—as I tried to sleep. This is fine, I thought. The tube might come out tomorrow. I can do this.

But the tube stayed in for a full week, and I lingered in the cardiac ICU five days because the pulmonary ICU was filled with COVID-19 patients, and then was transferred to a step-down unit for four nights, before Gary picked me up outside the same entrance where he had dropped me off the week before, unable to come inside the whole time because of the pandemic.

The cancer had spread to one of seventeen lymph nodes the surgeon removed along with a lobe of my left lung, necessitating four rounds of chemo and plummeting my five-year survival rate to 35 percent. Four rounds of chemo meant months on short-term disability from church in a time when they needed me most because everything was shut down before slowly reopening in limited ways. Some parishioners sent get-well cards asking me if we would be able to sing in church again before Christmas. Singing spread droplets, so at that time all hymns were instrumental only. I just watched them online from home, as I was not allowed to go anywhere but the infusion center. Others sent emails complaining about reopening procedures that were out of my control. "I knew you'd want to know," one beloved parishioner wrote. She was wrong. I just wanted to sleep, not vomit, and food to stop tasting like metal.

Gary cut my hair short after my first infusion because it was supposed to fall out. My family in Arizona couldn't be with me at all during this time, so they buzzed their heads in solidarity. This action meant more to me than any cards or prayers, but my own hair never fell out. "You bitch," one of my sisters laughed. "Now you have the longest hair in the family."

ANOTHER SICK STORY: IN THE ICU WITH THE DESERT MOTHERS

SAMANTHA

At church, we were still in the season of Christmas on January 2. Everyone else was taking down decorations as we continued to revel in the beauty of the poinsettias and slightly dried-out evergreens. I usually love the Sunday after Christmas. The chaos is over and I am free to worship. There is quiet. But this Sunday was different. Over the course of three hours presiding over services at church, my leg grew more and more painful. At noon, I hobbled out St. John's white front door wondering how a gentle hike had caused me so much pain. I was embarrassed at how out of shape I was. I came home and took a nap, which was a luxury with a five-year-old who gave up naps at age three. After my nap, I wanted to take several muscle relaxants and stay in bed, but I had an essay to finish before midnight about the desert mothers.

I was not familiar with the desert mothers when I'd been assigned this subject for a Christian blog. I remembered reading the desert fathers in seminary but had no memory of the desert mothers. Yet the January 5 feast day in the Episcopal Church recognizes three of these desert mothers: Syncletica of Alexandria, Theodora of the desert, and Sarah of the desert. All three of these women went by the title of *amma* (spiritual mother) and lived in the fourth and fifth centuries. All three went to the desert to become closer to God. The piece I was writing focused mostly on Amma Sarah because I found her to be the strangest and most intriguing.

Amma Sarah was the most isolated of the three. She was known for fighting the "demon of fornication" for thirteen years. One might wonder why that particular demon would be a challenge for a woman living alone in the desert, but apparently she was fighting not just the action but the thoughts. She sought purity of mind. She lived by a river for sixty years and never looked at it, because she was so intent on creating a union with God. She didn't want any distraction. Her desperation to rid herself of distraction made me uncomfortably aware of my need for distraction. I realized that I was always listening to an audiobook, a podcast, or music. Five minutes of silence was almost unbearable to me. I vowed in that piece to take five minutes a day to be silent. I was pretty sure I would fail, but I was going to try, damn it.

I took more muscle relaxants before bed, but they didn't help the pain. I only slept for a few hours. I woke covered in sweat with a swollen leg. I tried stretching, heat, ibuprofen, and nothing helped. The next night I tried to sleep on the floor of the living room, desperate to find a position that would relieve some pain. When I was still awake at three, I asked my husband, Conor, to take me to the emergency room.

It wasn't a pulled muscle: it was MRSA, and I was already septic. No one knew how I contracted it, but I was deathly ill by the time I got to the ER. Conor was allowed to wheel me in but could not stay in the waiting room. It was the peak of the Omicron variant's spike; no visitors allowed. This caused me to panic, as I wasn't sure I could even stay upright. The drunk man to my right moved over so I could lay across two seats. You know it's bad when the drunk people take pity on you. When they couldn't read my blood pressure because it was so low and realized my heart rate was 160, they brought me to the back. Conor was allowed to join me once I had a room. The pain was unbearable. A physician's assistant looked me in the eye and said, "You are very sick." I later learned what that really means is, "You might die." I was admitted to the ICU, where I stayed for six days.

They gave me strong narcotics and at least five different antibiotics, which gave me enough relief to sleep for a few hours at a time, but that wasn't enough sleep. Once the pain eased, the anxiety took over. People would call or text and ask me if I was catching up on my Netflix. I wanted to slap them. I couldn't do anything. All I could do was stare at the ceiling. I stared at the ceiling for hours with no sound but the beeping of monitors.

I heard music. One day I asked the nurse, "Who is playing U2 incessantly?" She had no idea who U2 was and assured me that there was no music. I silently cursed the generation that didn't know U2. She told me auditory hallucinations were common in the ICU. I wished they weren't. I had hoped God was trying to get through to me via Bono. I tried the Jesus Prayer: *Lord Jesus Christ, Son of God, have mercy on me, a sinner*. It brought me no comfort. I didn't feel like a sinner in need of mercy. I felt like a sick person in need of healing.

My second night, I prayed for a vision like the desert mothers had. I hadn't eaten or slept. I was stuck in a small room about the size of a monastic cell. I was basically an ascetic. I deserved a vision! I strained my eyes, and I thought I might be seeing Amma Sarah standing in the corner. I could only have visitors a few hours a day, and I was desperate for company, even a vision of a long-dead desert mother. She didn't stay long, which made me unexpectedly angry. I couldn't even get a vision to stay with me? When I'd read about her only days before, I found her a little crazy. Now, lying on that glorified air mattress of a hospital bed in a hospital gown and diaper, I felt just as crazy as she was. Yet my craziness wasn't bringing me any closer to God. God was moving farther away, and the scariest part was that I didn't even care. The desert mothers said that the cell was a place of spiritual combat.* If this was combat, I was losing.

In my first few days in the ICU, I prayed to have the attitude of a desert mother. They exalted suffering and thought it could bring them closer to God. I was suffering physically. Why was I so angry and depressed? Why was this not an opportunity to achieve unity with God? My prayers went unanswered, and if I am honest, they were far from sincere.

The desert mothers didn't merit their own book apparently, but *Sayings of the Desert Fathers* includes some of their words. Amma Sarah was known to have said, "I put out my foot to ascend the ladder, and I place death before my eyes before going up it."** Ascending a ladder was a common metaphor at the time for drawing closer to God. The desert mothers and fathers believed that the anticipation of death was not a depressing thing. Instead, it frees us to make different choices that help us live more in union with God.

Unfortunately, the prospect of death didn't help my relationship with God, further proof that I was never cut out to be an ascetic. It did teach me something: I didn't want to die. As someone who had poured out a bottle of pills in my

* Laura Swan, *The Forgotten Desert Mothers: Sayings, Lives, and Stories of Early Christian Women* (Mahwah, NJ: Paulist, 2013), 13.
** Swan, *The Forgotten Desert Mothers*, 39.

hand several times over the course of my life just to feel the possibility of death, this was a welcome realization. I hoped that, one day, that realization would help me. But in the hospital and the months after, the desire to live made me more anxious. Death is so much scarier when you realize how much you want to live. I wondered if the desert mothers wanted to live.

After five days of antibiotics, the number of my white blood cells was still dangerously high, which meant the infection had not abated. My dad was with me when the surgeon explained that they would have to open my leg and flush out the infection. I still couldn't move my leg, and they were worried that the infection had caused permanent damage. My dad tried to comfort me by saying, "You know, Bob Dole had permanent damage to the muscles in his arms. He just held on to that pen and he was fine." My dad is the most positive person I know, and even the ICU couldn't get him down, but there was no way I was going to be cheered up by visions of Bob Dole and his pen.

"It's my leg, Dad. I can't just hold a pen. I might not be able to walk, let alone run or do yoga. How am I supposed to keep up with a five-year-old with only one working leg?"

Fearing my dad might try for another inspirational talk, I asked him to read prayers out of the Book of Common Prayer. It was the first time I had tried to pray since my brief interaction with Amma Sarah and my insincere prayers to be like the desert mothers. I wept as he read them. My Catholic father reading out of the Episcopal prayer book was too much for me to bear. I was reminded of him reading at my ordination. I always loved the sound of his voice reading Scripture. It was his voice that gave me comfort. The words of praise and thanksgiving left me hollow. It was the last time I prayed until I left the hospital.

After one week and one surgery, I was out of the ICU and transferred to a regular room, which felt like what I imagined the Ritz would be. It smelled better than the ICU. There were fewer monitors, and my dinner came at five instead of eight. I still spent far too much time staring at the wall, but I also watched Netflix a little. I couldn't read yet, at least nothing more than a few sentences. Even *People* magazine seemed overwhelming to me. Sleep deprivation jumbled the words too much. My husband—who is a priest at an Episcopal church two towns over—brought me a card from one of his parishioners. I opened it and read the all-too-familiar "get well fast" message and threw it back at him. He picked it up and said, "They pray for you every day."

"I don't care. There is no point. The prayers aren't working." I knew my words were cruel and very unpriestly, but I didn't have the emotional stamina to stop the feelings that were coursing through my body.

Conor looked offended. "You are alive."

"Yeah, I guess." The cards continued to come, and I collected all of them in a large bag. It took me a while to read them. The weight of them brought me comfort, not the words. I would hold them in my hand and feel the weight of the prayers.

After two weeks I went home. I got in the bed of the study/playroom/guest room on the first floor of our house. I stared at the ceiling, and it was good to see a new ceiling. I patted the spot next to me and prayed, "Please stay with me tonight, Holy Spirit. I am scared and I am still alone. Please lay right here so I can feel your presence. Thank you for keeping me alive. I am sorry I didn't say thank you before, but thank you. Please stay." The anxiety kept me awake most of the night, but that prayer reminded me that the spiritual side of me was still there.

I am nothing like the desert mothers, yet I could not help but acknowledge the irony of my situation. Two weeks before, I couldn't imagine five minutes of silence, and now I was spending hours staring at the walls and ceilings. My husband would walk in the room and ask me what I was doing. "I am just staring at the wall. It's what I do now." Three days after my return home, I was back in the hospital again. The infection was not yet finished with me. I had one more surgery and was in the hospital for two more weeks before being discharged again. This time, I didn't pray at all. I just watched *Ted Lasso* and thanked the people who were praying for me. The prayers of others carried me while I was in the hospital. I couldn't pray, but I knew others were. I just hoped they weren't praying for patience. I had far too much practice with that.

1

PAIN AND ANGER

As Episcopal priests, we both turned to the Episcopal Book of Common Prayer in our illnesses. We had carried this prayer book with us when visiting critically ill people in the hospital or on hospice. But when praying for ourselves during each of our encounters with serious illness, some of its beautiful words rang hollow. The prayer "For the Sanctification of Illness," for example, one of two prayers Elizabeth had frequently prayed years before when her father was in chronically poor health, grated: "that the sense of her weakness may add strength to her faith and seriousness to her repentance."* Maybe having this chest tube inside my body can help me imagine Christ on the cross, Elizabeth hoped, trying to conjure up some way to "sanctify" this agony.

On the following page of the Book of Common Prayer, the prayer for pain says, "sustain me by your grace, that my strength and courage may not fail."**

* Book of Common Prayer, 1979, 460.
** Book of Common Prayer, 1979, 461.

People commend us for our courage when we're very ill, but it's not like we have a choice. Samantha thought about how she could either endure the pain or kill herself. She thought the pain had peaked when she was septic and could not move her leg, but two weeks later when they removed her first wound vacuum, she felt her courage fail. As they peeled the tape off her raw red leg she started to cry and begged them to stop as the tape took pieces of her skin with it. She didn't think her leg could take any more pain. She was mortified to have her courage fail just because someone was peeling tape off her leg. After all she had been through, how was this the thing that would break her? She needed more than God's grace in that moment, so she called her big brother and told him what happened. "Please tell me I am brave." She just needed to hear it.

In our experience as priests, we have observed that our parishioners feel guilty about expressing anger, especially to God. We've encouraged them to embrace the psalms, which often express anger as well as pain and misery. We both found the psalms, contained in the prayer book, to be more helpful than the other prayers, and it comforted us to know that Jesus prayed these psalms from the cross. Many of these psalms, however, are not prayed on Sundays in our usual cycle of readings, so churchgoers may not be as familiar with psalms of lament (or cursing) as they are with other psalms.

The first psalm in this section on pain is a variation on the first third of Psalm 22, which we hope will enable people to pray the actual psalm effectively.

VARIATION ON PSALM 22

My God who heals, why have you abandoned me?
And are so distant from my attempts to pray
and my groans of lament.

I cry out when the sun hits my eyes and
I am not ready to rise but you are silent;
and at night from the dark, when rest eludes me
and anxiety gnaws at me.

Yet you are the holy one,
praised by churchgoers every week.
They've praised you from those same sanctuaries
    for centuries
and you rescue them again and again.
When they call, you answer;
they trust you and you don't disappointment them.

But I'm lying here like a damn worm.
None of them, or anyone else, pays any attention to me.

Some mock me because I still believe in you
despite my agony.
If I believe in you, why am I in such pain?
"Where's your God now?" they smirk.
Some won't say it aloud but they wonder.

Faith was easier when I was young,
before my current pain.
There was a time when I felt safe,
when I trusted that you were my God.

Stay close now, please, God,
because I'm hurt and alone, and nothing helps. Amen.

PRAYER FOR WHEN
YOU CANNOT PRAISE

Why are you cast down, O my soul,
and why are you disquieted within me?
Hope in God; for I shall again praise him,
my help and my God.

—PSALM 42:11*

Dear God, today the hospital chaplain asked me if maybe I was depressed because I told her I cry every day. Do you think? Do you think after weeks in this God-forsaken place I might just be depressed? Do you think the relentless pain, the inability to walk, and the constant loneliness might just be making me depressed? God, I know why I am cast down. I know why my soul is disquieted. Do you? I always thought you understood our pain, but I am starting to wonder. I don't know that I will be able to praise you if I don't get better. I am supposed to praise you no matter what. But I am not sure I can. I don't have that kind of strength. I want to be that person who can praise God when I am sick and depressed, but right now, all I can do I is beg you to make me better. Let that be enough, God. Let my desperate pleas be enough praise for you. Amen.

---

* Unless otherwise indicated, Scripture verses in this book come from the New Revised Standard Version.

PRAYER FOR WHEN
YOU CAN'T PRAY

> Likewise the Spirit helps us in our weakness, for we do not know how to pray as we ought, but that very Spirit intercedes with sighs too deep for words.
>
> –ROMANS 8:26

Dear God, I can't. I can't pray. I can't bear another moment of this agony. Make me numb to the pain because these narcotics aren't doing it. I can't pray because I can't form words. Paul writes that the Spirit intercedes with sighs too deep for words. Holy Spirit, intercede with those holy sighs. I can only weep at my own weakness. Bless my tears. May they be a balm. If you can't free me from pain, let these tears free me from shame. Amen.

PRAYER FOR BETTER ANSWERS

God, you know how they say that "God always answers prayer, he just doesn't always say yes." That used to make sense to me. I didn't like it, but it explained some things. But when you are sick and you pray to get better, that explanation sucks. Just make me better. That's an easy yes, God, for everyone involved. Just answer yes. Amen.

PRAYER FOR MORE
PRODUCTIVE SUFFERING

> And not only that, but we also boast in our sufferings, knowing that suffering produces endurance, and endurance produces character, and character produces hope, and hope does not disappoint us, because God's love has been poured into our hearts through the Holy Spirit that has been given to us.
>
> —ROMANS 5:3–5

Dear Holy Spirit, I think I need some more of that love you are supposed to pour into my heart. My suffering isn't producing any endurance, and if I can't endure, how will I get to character and hope? I am okay skipping character, but I would really like to get to that hope part. Please, God, pour your love into my heart because I don't have the strength to endure this on my own. Amen.

PRAYER FOR FORGIVENESS
FOR WHAT I SAID WHILE IN PAIN

Dear God, I think that swearing when in pain shouldn't count against me. In fact, no words said when in enormous pain should count against me, even words against you. Or perhaps you could just provide some automatic forgiveness. If there is no such thing as automatic forgiveness—then I am sorry, God. I didn't mean it. Amen.

PRAYER FOR NUMBNESS

My God, my God, why have you forsaken me? IT HURTS. It hurts so much. I can't move; I can't lie still. I can't smile when people come into the room. I cannot bear this. Please, just bring numbness. Let me breathe without wincing. Wipe my mind clear. Free me from the anger that burns at you and everyone else because I am in this place. Amen.

PRAYER FOR SLEEP

A great windstorm arose, and the waves beat into the boat, so that the boat was already being swamped. But he was in the stern, asleep on the cushion; and they woke him up and said to him, "Teacher, do you not care that we are perishing?"

−MARK 4:37–38

Jesus, you slept on a cushion while a windstorm raged and waves beat the boat and your disciples wondered why you didn't care that they were about to perish. I will perish without sleep. Rebuke my pain, Lord, and calm my mind. Let me breathe in ease, rest, tranquility, and breathe out throbbing, agony, ache. Create the dead calm in me that you made of the sea. Amen.

PRAYER OF PRAISE FOR RELEASE

Dear Holy Spirit, I am not the kind of Christian who loudly praises you, not even in church. I am not the kind of Christian who says "praise God" when something good happens. Maybe I should be, but I am not. Today I was. When they took me out of the MRI machine and unstrapped me from that unforgiving board, I praised you. I will always remember the relief I felt when being released from that damn board, the relief that you were denied when hanging on the cross. Thank you for that feeling of freedom that so many people are denied. Amen.

PRAYER ABOUT PAINKILLERS

Jesus, who was in more pain on the cross than I can imagine: I need these pills but am petrified of addiction. Books and movies show dire endings that started with taking them for three days. What am I supposed to do? If I take them, do I know when to stop? Please help calm my thoughts and keep me from addiction and pain. Let the pills soothe my pain and not lead me down a path of destruction. Amen.

PRAYER FOR COURAGE
IN THE MIDST OF PAIN

Dear Jesus, who suffered on the cross, all I can think about now is pain, my pain. I see it. I feel it. I smell it. I don't care what anyone else is thinking or feeling. Right now, all I know is pain and the desperate desire that it end. How did you forgive people when you hung on the cross bleeding and suffocating? How did you love others with that kind of overwhelming pain? The only person I can forgive is the person bringing me the painkillers. Please, God, give me some courage and compassion in the midst of my pain. Remind me that I am not the only one hurting and this pain cannot last forever. It won't, will it? Please tell me it will end. Amen.

PRAYER FOR ANGER

> Then Jesus entered the temple and drove out all who were
> selling and buying in the temple, and he overturned the
> tables of the money changers and the seats of those who
> sold doves.
>
> —MATTHEW 21:12

Dear Jesus, who turned over the tables in the temple, I want to
be angry. I have always admired the depth of your emotions—
the way you felt anger, sadness, and joy. You experienced all of
human emotions so that we could pray to you and you would
understand. Right now, I am too weary and depressed to feel
much of anything. I want to be angry at you because that
would mean I still cared. I don't think I care about you right
now. I have forgotten how to talk to you, even in anger. The fact
that I don't care scares me the most, God. I am not angry at you
because you don't matter enough to me. Please, God, help me
be angry. Amen.

BLESSING FOR HEALTH-CARE WORKERS WHO MAKE CARELESS REMARKS

God, bless the tech who told me that her grandmother died from my disease. I pray for her grandmother's soul and her grief. I also pray that she never says that to another person. Amen.

PRAYER FOR JEALOUSY

Our anger at our own frustration, and our envy of those
more fortunate than ourselves, We confess to you, Lord.

—LITANY OF PENITENCE, ASH WEDNESDAY SERVICE,
BOOK OF COMMON PRAYER, 267

I the LORD your God am a jealous God.

—EXODUS 20:5B

God, who is a jealous God: sometimes I am so jealous of others
that I feel physical pain: not just those who casually stroll down
the street staring at their phone in one hand with a cigarette
in the other and a dog on a long leash, or the ones laughing
without a mask in a class at the gym, but even the ones who
are just a little less sick than I am. I'm stunned by the venom
I feel. Cleanse my heart, God. Also, please make them a little
less careless and a bit more thankful for the ease at which they
move in the world. Amen.

PRAYER OF ANGER ABOUT THINGS WE AREN'T SUPPOSED TO THINK ABOUT

> Finally, beloved, whatever is true, whatever is honorable, whatever is just, whatever is pure, whatever is pleasing, whatever is commendable, if there is any excellence and if there is anything worthy of praise, think about these things.
>
> —PHILIPPIANS 4:8

Jesus, who suffered much more than I do, I love the verse from Philippians that implores us to think about whatever is true and honorable, just, pure, pleasing, commendable, excellent, and worthy of praise. I also wonder what Paul would have thought of others using it to try to cheer up people like me who are sick. Thoughts of other things creep in, like Scotland and Chile and places I haven't been, jobs I will likely never have now, marathons I will never run. I want to be positive, but I need some anger first. Let me be angry. Let me not care if my anger scares other people. Amen.

2

BLOOD AND BREATH

I (Samantha) was only supposed to be attached to a wound vacuum for one week. I ended up with four different wound vacs over the course of three months. If you have not experienced the joy of a wound vac, imagine a suction cup taped to an open wound on your body with a tube coming out attached to a small machine. In the hospital, the machine is the size of a briefcase and isn't portable. If you are lucky enough to leave the hospital with a wound vac, it comes in a smaller size that you can carry on your shoulder, like a messenger bag. For the first several weeks that I was attached to the portable wound vac, I was too weak to leave the house except for doctors appointments. About three weeks into my fourth wound vac, I decided to venture out periodically, careful to cover the tube that my blood flowed slowly through. A physical therapist came to my house twice a week, and I was eventually able to talk to her about my return to work.

"I just feel weird, walking down the aisle in church with this contraption on my leg. I hate the idea of my parishioners seeing my blood. It's just gross."

The therapist looked at me and said, "Is that necessarily a bad thing? Isn't blood a symbol of life, and wouldn't that be a powerful reminder for the people in your parish?"

"Well, that's a good point." I will be damned, I thought. I just got schooled in theology by my physical therapist. While she had an excellent point, I still didn't think I could return to my position as rector of a parish with a machine sucking my blood. We talk about the blood of Christ in church every time we celebrate communion. When we present the chalice to those who are kneeling at the rail, we say, "The blood of Christ, the cup of salvation." Episcopalians have mixed opinions on the sacrament. Most of us don't believe it actually becomes the blood of Christ. We believe that it has changed in some tangible way, and that it has become the cup of salvation. Perhaps if I was in a Catholic church I would be more comfortable with a tube carrying my blood, since Catholics believe the sacrament is the blood of Christ. But in the Episcopal Church, I fear that the sacrament has become more of a symbol, and less . . . well, less bloody.

I waited until I was free of the wound vac and able to walk without a cane before returning to church. It was partly because I didn't have the strength to return. It was also because I wasn't ready for people to see me as wounded. It was bad enough that my son, my husband, my parents, and countless medical professionals have seen my open wound. I wasn't ready for the people in my parish to see that.

Elizabeth and I decided to call this section "Blood and Breath." I had a lot of feelings about wounds and scars, and Elizabeth had much to say about breath.

Both of these things are themes throughout the Bible, and even in worship. We talk about blood in relation to the blood of Christ. When we talk about breath, it's usually associated with the Holy Spirit. Both are needed to live. When we bleed and when we struggle for breath, we can't help but feel incredibly vulnerable.

Maybe that was really why I didn't want to go to church with a wound vac. I wasn't ready to be vulnerable. I have always valued emotional vulnerability. However, being vulnerable physically is a much different thing. In my experience, emotional vulnerability was a choice I made. I could display it or hide it. However, if you are bleeding or can't breathe—that's not vulnerability that you can hide. Suddenly your weakness is on display. Even after my wound vac was removed, I still wore a massive bandage, which would leak. Once I made the mistake of wearing white pants to church, and I felt like I just got my period for the first time, in front of my staff. It wasn't until my wound healed that I felt comfortable again. I want to tell you how fortunate I am that I am no longer vulnerable in that way. I know that I am fortunate. Yet being ill teaches you that every person is vulnerable—we are just vulnerable in varying degrees. That is one of the astounding things about the Christian faith. We believe in a God who chose to take a human body and become physically vulnerable. God made this choice so we could pray to God knowing that God understands our pain. God knows what it is to bleed in front of people, to struggle for breath, and to weep. That's a God worth praying to.

PRAYER FOR WOUNDS

Dear God, I have always loved that Jesus's resurrected body bore the scars of his crucifixion. It showed he was vulnerable and human. But, God, wounds don't heal that quickly. Wounds like that bleed for days, weeks, maybe even months. I know this, as I have bled for months, and I have no scar. I pray for a scar. God, please give me a scar. I would gladly take a scar over a weeping and bloody wound. Amen.

PRAYER FOR MY WOUND VAC

Dear Jesus, you had nails in your hands and feet and a spear in your side. It was three hours of agony. I have had this machine attached to me for months. It's not agony, but it's pretty damn annoying. Please ease my anxiety when the nurse pulls it out to clean my wound. May my ears be deaf to the giant sucking sound the machine makes as it is removed from my raw skin. Give me the courage to look at the wound without hyperventilating. Please help me when the suction cup falls off in the middle of the night and makes noise that sounds like a dying animal. Jesus, I hate seeing the blood in the clear tube. I hate being aware of my blood and my wound all the time. Let me know this is not forever, that I will one day walk without this burden strapped to me. It's not a cross—it's a handy bag, but I still hate it. Free me from the bag, but also give me perspective. Amen.

Then he said to Thomas, "Put your finger here and see my hands. Reach out your hand and put it in my side. Do not doubt but believe."

—JOHN 20:27

Dear Jesus, who showed off his scars, thank you for healing, for closed wounds that no longer seep. Thank you for no more bandages and wound nurses and wound vacuums. I may feel that my scar is long and ugly, but it tells my story: a story of pain and hard work. I am still wounded. But alive. No one will need to touch my scar for assurance of my corporal being, as they did yours, but I will. And I will remember the strength you gave me, the strength to survive. Amen.

ANOTHER PRAYER ABOUT SCARS

Jesus, who showed his holes to Thomas: people can't see all my scars and discoloration so they think I'm fine, but I'm not. I can't believe that stuff about weather changes and scars is true. I can't believe that people forget what happened to me and think I am the same. Unchanged. Some might believe that they honor me with high expectations, but I hate their high expectations and doubt I can do what they want. Does this doubt bother you? Don't you think you were a little hard on Thomas? Help me to be hopeful and fair, and them to be realistic and reasonable. Amen.

PRAYER FOR BETTER VEINS

Dear Jesus, I am weary of the needles. They take my blood. They give me blood. They give me medicine. They hydrate me—always with needles. I used to have big beautiful veins that nurses would compliment me on. Now they look at them and seem to judge me, like it's my fault they went bad. It's my fault they have to call a specialist. I apologize because that is what I do. Jesus, please give me courage as they stab at me repeatedly. May I not resent the person who is doing the stabbing. Also, could you please give me my plump and robust veins back? Amen.

THANKSGIVING FOR BLOOD

And he did the same with the cup after supper, saying,
"This cup that is poured out for you is the new covenant
in my blood."

–LUKE 22:20

Dear Jesus, who offered us your body and blood, thank you for
the stranger's blood that is coursing through my body. I am
grateful for this gift of life, but it feels too intimate. Someone
else's blood is in my body. I didn't have a choice. I had to take
it. I wonder if that was how the disciples felt when you offered
them your blood. Did they accept it with ease? Thank you for
the gift of your blood, God. When I consume the wine from the
chalice, let me remember this moment—what it is to receive
life-giving blood. Amen.

PRAYER FOR ALL KINDS
OF BODILY FLUIDS

> In his anguish he prayed more earnestly, and his sweat became like great drops of blood falling down on the ground.
>
> —LUKE 22:44

Dear Jesus, who suffered even while praying, we talk a lot about your suffering. Well, some of us do. Lately I have been thinking about you praying in Gethsemane and begging God to take the cup from you. You sweat blood. This image has always disturbed me, but after sweating and bleeding at the same time, I understood what that must have felt like. Blood is gross by itself, but when it mixes with other bodily fluids, it's unbearable. You must have been in agony if you were sweating blood. So you understand my agony as my body deteriorates. You understand the pain, and the grossness. I am grateful for your understanding. But really, God, I would like you to take the blood and sweat away and then get me a shower, because I really smell. Amen.

HOLY SPIRIT AND BREATH

Holy Spirit, whose name is Breath: fill my broken body with your being. Let me breathe in love, strength, patience, awe. Exhale rage, pain, helplessness. While I breathe, make yourself known to me all the way to my fingertips, even when my breath catches on something that hurts; even when I can't take a full, deep breath. Release me from my fear of breathing. Amen.

VARIATIONS ON
THE JESUS BREATH PRAYER

Original:

Inhale: Lord Jesus Christ, Son of God
Exhale: Have mercy on me, a sinner.

Inhale: Christ, who suffered on a cross,
Exhale: Remind me that I'm a badass.

Inhale: Spirit that breathed over earth,
Exhale: Let me exhale without a catch.

Inhale: Jesus, who healed all he saw,
Exhale: Release me from pain and anger.

PRAYER ABOUT THIS CHEST TUBE

He makes wars cease to the end of the earth;
    he breaks the bow, and shatters the spear;
    he burns the shields with fire.

—PSALM 46:9

God, who breaks the bow and shatters the spear: please do
something about this chest tube. The surgeon said it "might" be
"uncomfortable." Has he ever been subjected to a tube coming
out of a chest cavity collecting fluid into a small suitcase? How
can I have conversations with the people who come by with
this thing sticking out of me? How will they see me as someone
with dreams and friends and important work when liquids are
seeping out before their eyes? I know I should praise the person who invented this device so that I can heal and eventually
breathe better. So, fine: praise them. You created people: thank
you, Lord! Praise you. But please banish the word "discomfort"
from their vocabularies and get this tube out of me, soon, and
not because I died or because it fell out. Get it out and let it
stay out. Amen.

CURSING PRAYER FOR
THE SPIROMETER

> When he had said this, he breathed on them and said to them, "Receive the Holy Spirit."
>
> —JOHN 20:22

Dear Jesus, who breathed on your disciples, why did you do that? Was it because your breath is holy? I never really appreciated how holy breath was until I didn't have it. It seems I never have enough breath. They have given me this horrible plastic device called a spirometer. What a ridiculous name. I am told that I need to do this every hour or I will get pneumonia. I already have enough problems and I really don't need any more illnesses, but I hate this device. Every time I do it I feel like I am failing a test for a class that I never attended. And, God, I always went to my classes. I am always prepared and in control, and I hate that I cannot control this spirometer or anything else in my life. Jesus, breathe on me. May that breath give me the endurance I lack. May it give me the peace you promised your disciples when you breathed on me so that I can release my need for control. Then suck the breath out of the people who want to lecture me about this damn spirometer . . . not to hurt them, just to keep them from lecturing me. Amen.

PRAYER FOR
A DEEP, PAINLESS BREATH

For he crushes me with a tempest,
    and multiplies my wounds without cause;
he will not let me get my breath,
    but fills me with bitterness.

—JOB 9:17–18

Dear Holy Spirit, I am scared to breathe. I know that breathing deeply helps with anxiety and all sorts of things. The deep breaths are painful. My body feels as though it is being crushed when I move away from my shallow and safe breathing. When I breathe deeply, I get a piercing pain in my chest and I wonder if this is how I am going to die. Is this an anxiety attack or is my heart giving out? Holy Spirit, I know that there are a lot of nice things about breath in the Bible, but all I can think of right now is the pain that breathing is causing me. Let me get my breath. When I exhale, let me exhale the bitterness that has built up in me. Amen.

PRAYER ASKING GOD
TO BREATHE FOR ME

> Then the LORD God formed man from the dust of the ground, and breathed into his nostrils the breath of life; and the man became a living being.
>
> —GENESIS 2:7

God, who blew into Adam's nostrils: I'm sick of struggling to breathe. I will continue with the cursed spirometer, but please, please breathe into my nostrils like you did for Adam so that I stay a living being. I'm exhausted and need your help, your breath. Amen.

BREATH TERROR

> Then the LORD God formed man from the dust of the ground, and breathed into his nostrils the breath of life; and the man became a living being
>
> —GENESIS 2:7

> Then Jesus cried again with a loud voice and breathed his last.
>
> —MATTHEW 27:50

Creator, who breathed life into Adam: breathe something into me, because with this disease I wheeze and gasp and avoid oximeters. I worry I will not eventually fade away in peace but will die with my mouth open struggling to draw breath. When I used to read about Jesus or Abraham or Ishmael or Isaac or Jacob breathing their last, it sounded dignified, but I imagine myself red-faced, eyes wide in terror, with a gurgle instead of a loud voice. Please don't let me die that way. Amen.

LAMENT FOR THE LACK OF LUNG METAPHORS IN THE BIBLE

And the LORD was sorry that he had made humankind on the earth, and it grieved him to his heart.

—GENESIS 6:6

Rend your hearts and not your clothing.

—JOEL 2:13A

Circumcise, then, the foreskin of your heart, and do not be stubborn any longer.

—DEUTERONOMY 10:16

But I say to you that everyone who looks at a woman with lust has already committed adultery with her in his heart.

—MATTHEW 5:28

For where your treasure is, there your heart will be also.

—MATTHEW 6:21

God, who inspired the Bible that bursts with metaphors about the heart: Where are images about lungs? In Scripture people rend their hearts and circumcise the foreskins of their hearts, but there's nothing about lungs. Hearts hold treasure and can get us into trouble. Even you have a heart, according to Genesis. What about lungs—do you have those, too? I only have one now and am terrified that something will happen to it. I keep my distance from people to keep that lung safe, but when I turn to the Bible for companionship, it only talks to me about hearts. Is my lung lonely without the other one? What emotions does it hold? I want more words for what I lost when the tumor-ridden lung was taken. Amen.

3

WAITING, WANDERING, AND WONDERING

In our experience, being seriously sick takes longer than anyone lets on at first. Sometimes we wait months for a diagnosis, and sometimes we linger in the hospital for weeks, or our time away is much longer than we would have thought possible. Extended illness can be boring. A few weeks into chemo, I (Elizabeth) posted something about fighting cancer being boring. A couple of people took me to task for this: "Trust me, you don't want it to be exciting," one said. I wanted to point out that I'd had a lot of excitement, being diagnosed with two primary cancers within three months of each other, causing several surgeries plus radiation and now chemo. Another woman scolded and then unfriended me. Still, I stand by my feeling. So much of chemo and radiation consisted of waiting, and I became bored. I mostly lay on the couch or slumped in a recliner. I had trouble writing or doing any of the things I love. Once I took four naps in one day.

Most of the waiting, however, produced extreme anxiety. What would these nodules turn out to be?

What would the various scans and biopsies and "procedures" reveal? Was I going to die soon? Would I be able to keep working? Would I lose my hair, even my eyebrows and eyelashes? What would breathing feel like after the surgery?

"Try not to think about it" was unhelpful, but of course, in prayer I pleaded with God to help me not to think about it. My husband suggested short bursts of thinking about it, like during my morning walks while playing music. That was an outlet, but I never achieved a state of not thinking about results when waiting. One of the psalmists best reflected my feeling, writing in Psalm 69,

> I am weary with my crying;
>> my throat is parched.
> My eyes grow dim
>> with waiting for my God.

Every scan meant waiting, and sometimes I had to wait to get the scan scheduled. Sometimes I felt like nothing happened unless I nagged people, which made me feel guilty and I wondered how people who weren't willing to do this managed to make anything happen.

Wandering feels like a punishment, like the Israelites wandering in the wilderness for forty years until a whole generation had died. After my initial surgeries, radiation, and chemotherapy, I felt like I was wandering in the wilderness between scans to see if that treatment had worked. After a year there were new nodules, so the scans would be a check to see if they were stable. Eventually, they were not, and then I was back to waiting, but still wandering. Trying to move ahead with my life, my vocation and church, my writing, but not being clear about where I was going. Nothing was a straight line. The church labyrinth soothed me, since labyrinths are not mazes: one way in, one way out. They were used in lieu of long physical pilgrimages in ancient times. I don't know if I will ever travel again, but I can walk a labyrinth.

While walking and wandering I'm always wondering. Will I travel again? Will I be able to keep working? What will the church do if I have to retire early? When I was away on short-term disability, they were fine, which was a relief but then led to wondering if what I do matters. They don't need me—obviously. I'm not Jesus. But I wonder who I am without them. I wonder if the children in the church will remember me if I die soon. I wonder if my own great-nieces and great-nephews will remember me. I wonder what will happen to Gary. Will he stay in Virginia? Get married again? What will happen if his new wife gets sick? As we get older, this scenario we're living will happen again. If he gets ill first, will she take care of him as gently and lovingly as he has taken care of me?

And even though I would do all in my power to reassure anyone in my church who asked that the situation is not their fault, I still sometimes wonder, "What did I do? Why is this happening to me?"

LITANY OF UNBELIEF

> Jesus said to him, "If you are able!—All things can be done for the one who believes." Immediately the father of the child cried out, "I believe; help my unbelief!"
>
> —MARK 9:23–24

Dear Jesus,

I believe in miracles, but I don't believe they can happen to me. Help my unbelief.

I believe in prayer, but I am not sure how it all works. Help my unbelief.

I believe that it's not your fault when bad things happen, but I still blame you. Help my unbelief.

I believe that death is not the end, but I am reluctant to test that. Help my unbelief.

I believe I am brave and strong, but mostly I am afraid. Help my unbelief.

I believe that you are always with me, but I also feel lonely most of the time. Help my unbelief.

I believe in your love and unconditional grace, which is why I can admit these things. Help me believe. Amen.

ANTIPATIENCE PRAYER

Dear God, I am grateful for all the people who are praying for me. Really, I am. But please tell whoever is praying for patience to stop. Just stop. I am set with patience. Perhaps they could pray for time to speed up. That would be more helpful. Also, enough with the humility. Tell that prayer warrior to shut up. Amen.

SEEKING SOLACE IN SILENCE

He said, "Go out and stand on the mountain before the
Lord, for the Lord is about to pass by." Now there was a
great wind, so strong that it was splitting mountains and
breaking rocks in pieces before the Lord, but the Lord
was not in the wind; and after the wind an earthquake, but
the Lord was not in the earthquake; and after the earthquake a fire, but the Lord was not in the fire; and after the
fire a sound of sheer silence.

—1 KINGS 19:11–12

God, who appeared to Elijah not in an earthquake but in sheer
silence: help me to find you in the silence when techs leave the
room because a scan is starting. Call to me from the silence
between scans when waiting for results. Sit beside me in the
waiting room after two other patients have been called back
and their caregivers begin to speak about how brave they
are, how well they are doing, how difficult all this is. When I
struggle to stay silent myself, send a great wind or earthquake
or fire. Amen.

PRAYER ABOUT WAITING ROOMS

Wait for the LORD;
    be strong, and let your heart take courage;
wait for the LORD!

—PSALM 27:14

God, who seems to encourage waiting: I spend so much time in the waiting rooms, and so do my loved ones, who sometimes wait without me. How are our hearts supposed to take courage when our souls feel like they're being sucked out by the bland art on the walls, no doubt bought in bulk? Sometimes the waiting rooms have trees: for Christmas, for Valentine's Day, even pink in support of breast cancer. I detest these decorations that are supposed to distract and comfort. Help me breathe in strength and solace in waiting rooms. When my loved ones are alone in such rooms, let them feel Jesus next to them. Amen.

"Consider the lilies of the field, how they grow; they neither toil nor spin, yet I tell you, even Solomon in all his glory was not clothed like one of these. But if God so clothes the grass of the field, which is alive today and tomorrow is thrown into the oven, will he not much more clothe you—you of little faith?"

—MATTHEW 6:28-20

Jesus, do you remember when you said to consider the lilies of the field? I want you to know that I have considered them now, and it's not helping. It's not helping at all. My anxiety is so high that no allusion to flowers will accomplish a thing. Please, Jesus, give me more than lilies. Amen.

A LAMENT FOR MY BODY

Dear Jesus, most of the crucifixes I have seen are gruesome—yet, your body always appears perfectly sculpted, like you've been doing Crossfit and keto. But let me tell you, lying in a hospital bed for weeks is hell on the body. When I had the presence of mind to look at my body for the first time, I was horrified by what I saw. The muscles were gone. Jesus, I was never a perfect specimen, but I had muscles that I could see. They are gone, and I cannot help but lament the body I never appreciated and wonder if those muscles will ever come back. If they do, how long will it take? I can't imagine having the energy to rebuild my body. Please, give me the energy and the endurance I need to come back from this. The doctor tells me I will, but I don't believe *him*. Jesus, if you can come back from death, surely I can come back from this.

PRAYER FOR SCANXIETY

With the LORD on my side I do not fear.
What can mortals do to me?

—PSALM 118:6

Do not fear, for I am with you,
do not be afraid, for I am your God.

—ISAIAH 41:10A

The angel said to her, "Do not be afraid, Mary, for you have
found favor with God."

—LUKE 1:30

Holy Spirit, my body is tense and fraught while my mind wanders to the worst: guide the hands of the tech so that they find a vein swiftly. Help me to be still so that they take clear images. Let this scan be clear and the results swift. If something shows up, fill me with confidence because I have beaten this before. I am still here. Remind me of the mantra Do Not Fear. Fill me with calming peace. Amen.

PRAYER TO BE OKAY
WITH DOUBT

> The hand of the LORD came upon me, and he brought me out by the spirit of the LORD and set me down in the middle of a valley; it was full of bones. He led me all around them; there were very many lying in the valley, and they were very dry. He said to me, "Mortal, can these bones live?" I answered, "O Lord GOD, you know."
>
> —EZEKIEL 37:1-3

Dear God, I have been wondering this about myself lately— can these bones live? Not just the bones, God, but everything. If things don't get better, can I live like this? I don't know, and that troubles me. But, God, maybe I should be okay with Ezekiel's response to your question. Ezekiel was a prophet and he answered, "O Lord GOD, you know." That seems like the way prophets say, "I don't know." I have no idea if I have the strength to go on feeling the way I do. I have hope that things will get better, but that hope is surrounded by doubt. Sometimes the doubt wins. God, help me be okay with not knowing. Help me be okay with relying on your knowledge and your strength. O Lord God, you know. Right now, may that be enough. Amen.

PRAYER TO HURRY UP

I remember the devotion of your youth,
    your love as a bride,
how you followed me in the wilderness.

—JEREMIAH 2:2

Remember the long way that the LORD your God has led
you these forty years in the wilderness, in order to humble
you, testing you to know what was in your heart, whether
or not you would keep his commandments.

—DEUTERONOMY 8:2

God, in Jeremiah, you sound like you loved it when the Israelites were wandering in the desert for forty years. Heavenly Father, please understand that the rest of us hate it. We've read those other parts of the Bible where it's clear you made them wander around as a punishment. Stop punishing me. And you might want to protect those who tell me to be patient or live in the present from my simmering ball of rage. Prod the doctors to figure out what's next, fast. I know I am one of many impatient patients, but I must start moving toward a destination. Amen.

PRAYER WHEN TRYING TO SLEEP FOR AN HOUR BEFORE A PET SCAN

Here I am again, God, hungry with a sore arm after they filled me with fluid, and now I have to sit here for an hour without reading because that would draw the dye toward my eyes. So once again I am praying for sleep. Help me not to think about the damn scan and why I'm having it and what it will show. What should I count to help me sleep? Doctors? Disciples? Ways to be martyred? Jacob's sons? All the women who should have gotten more ink in the Bible? That last one irritates me too much to settle me down. Please, force sleep to submit to me. Amen.

PRAYER WHEN YOU HAVE TO LIE STILL FOR HOURS FOLLOWING A DIAGNOSTIC PROCEDURE

Lord, let me sleep so the time passes quickly. Let me not obsess over whatever it is they think might happen if I don't lie here in this narrow bed inside these blue curtains listening to people gurgle and belch around me. Time is nothing to you, so sweep it away so I can go home. Amen.

WHEN WAITING ON TESTS AND RESULTS

God, in the Bible you speak of the time that the Israelites were wandering in the desert with great longing. That was preincarnation, so maybe you don't get how it felt for them. I can assure you that it was awful. We humans hate uncertainty. I am having to wait weeks to figure out what is wrong with me and cannot fathom forty years of such nonsense. God, send me some clarity. Please. Amen.

PRAYER WHEN DISTRACTED

God, who created the world in seven days, I can't seem to create anything right now, or even pick up the phone to hire someone to do a simple and needed task in my house. All I can do is think of the upcoming test and its result. Please, God, help me to focus. Save me from platitudes of well-meaning loved ones. Dissipate my rage that covers concern. Let the days fly by so that I am on the other side of this, whatever the result. Grant me the gifts of sleep and strength. Amen.

PRAYER WHEN WAITING
TO SEE A DOCTOR

Now a certain man was ill, Lazarus of Bethany, the village of Mary and her sister Martha. Mary was the one who anointed the Lord with perfume and wiped his feet with her hair; her brother Lazarus was ill. So the sisters sent a message to Jesus, "Lord, he whom you love is ill." But when Jesus heard it, he said, "This illness does not lead to death; rather it is for God's glory, so that the Son of God may be glorified through it." Accordingly, though Jesus loved Martha and her sister and Lazarus, after having heard that Lazarus was ill, he stayed two days longer in the place where he was.

–JOHN 11:1-6

Dear Jesus, who waited to cure Lazarus, I know why you waited to cure Lazarus. You needed to show the people what you were capable of. It was a bit of a preview of the resurrection. I still struggle with the fact that you put his family and friends through that grief, but I can understand it. I am always waiting for doctors. I don't even ask them to come to me like you did for Lazarus—I go to them. Yet still, I wait. I wait in the waiting room. Then I wait again in the small room. I wait for tests and for consults. The problem is, if I die, these doctors can't bring me back to life. They need to see me when I am alive. Please help me endure the waiting and find ways to keep myself busy. Open my eyes when I am in the waiting room and let that be an opportunity to pray for the others who are there. They are waiting too. But if I am being totally honest, what I would really like is for you to talk to the doctors (or whoever makes these decisions) and tell them to stop overscheduling patients to make more money. Until then, open my heart to the suffering of those around me. Amen.

PRAYER TO LIE DOWN
IN THE EMERGENCY ROOM

> Just then some men came, carrying a paralyzed man on a
> bed. They were trying to bring him in and lay him before
> Jesus; but finding no way to bring him in because of the
> crowd, they went up on the roof and let him down with
> his bed through the tiles into the middle of the crowd in
> front of Jesus.
>
> —LUKE 5:18–19

Dear Jesus, who cured people when they were lying down,
why are the chairs in the emergency room so uncomfortable,
and why can't there be long benches? I can't sit up for another
moment. I need to lie down, and there is nowhere to lie down.
Apparently they frown on lying down on the floor. It doesn't
have to be comfortable, God. I just can't be vertical anymore.
You often cured people when they were lying down . . . because
that is what sick people do. Remember when you cured a man
because his friends lowered him through the roof on a bed? It
was a bed! You commended them on their faith. I would have
too. Those friends were awesome. But you know what is really
impressive—sitting in a chair in an emergency room when you
might be dying. I hope I got some faith commendation for that.
But more than a commendation, I just want a flat surface. Can
you make that happen? Amen.

PRAYER OF THANKS
FOR MY FRIENDS

Dear God, I have been thinking more about those awesome friends who lowered the sick man through the roof. I have friends who would do that, not many, but enough. I have friends who hold my hand when I cry and send me gummy bears. I have friends who send flowers, so many that every nurse and every doctor comments on them. I have friends who let me ask the hard questions. I have some friends who never say the right thing, but I have some who always know what to say. I thank you for both of those kinds of friends. Because no matter what they are saying, they still call and text and answer when I call. Thank you, God, for those dear friends. Amen.

PRAYER WHEN THE WAIT FOR A DIAGNOSIS IS FINALLY OVER

> Then he came to the disciples and found them sleeping; and he said to Peter, "So, could you not stay awake with me one hour?"
>
> —MATTHEW 26:40

Jesus, your disciples could not wait with you for one hour. Some say waiting is the worst. But even worse than waiting has been bad news after weeks of waiting, wandering, and wondering. I want to offer a prayer of thanksgiving that my wait is over, but I'm furious and scared and sad. So instead, please, just sit here with me. Amen.

4

HOSPITALS

My monthlong hospitalization in January 2022 was not my first hospital stay. I (Samantha) had been in the hospital for four days in my early thirties after complications with an infertility treatment. I remember the nurses being wonderful because they were excited to have someone their age, someone who was healthy enough to joke with about the extrawide wheelchair they wheeled me out in. That time, I could walk to the bathroom without an alarm going off. Anyone could visit. A family member stayed over every night. I never felt alone. I was scared and uncomfortable, but never alone.

This time, though, when I was told that I was in septic shock and would need to be admitted to the ICU, it was also the peak of the Omicron variant. The hospital staff was at the breaking point. Two nurses admitted to me that they were considering quitting. They didn't have enough staff to get me out of bed more than two to three times a day. For the first week, they had me in a diaper with some horrible contraption called a purewick. It is neither pure nor a wick, but it looks a bit like a candle and goes where no candle should go. It would have been funny if I wasn't peeing uncontrollably due to the amount of liquids they were pumping into me. I was later told that pumping massive amounts of liquid into someone's body is what they do when they are trying to revive that person.

We use water a lot in church as a symbol. When we have a baptism in the Episcopal Church, we provide a brief history of the symbolism of water. The Holy Spirit moved over the waters during creation and Moses divided the Red Sea, allowing the Hebrew people to escape from slavery. In the Bible, water gives life. I knew it was giving me life, but most of the time, I felt like I was drowning. I felt more like the Egyptians who were drowned in the water than the Hebrew people who escaped to the other side. When they did get me up and walk me across the room, I would have to take a break after six feet, I was so winded. One week prior, I was hiking. I would ask the nurse to carry my water cup so when I stopped, I could drink water. Despite the amount of liquid they were pumping through my system, I was thirsty all the time.

I asked a friend to bring me a Book of Common Prayer and a prayer shawl. I never opened the Book of Common Prayer. The prayer shawl brought me some comfort, but I was terrified I would accidentally pee on it, so it sat in the corner most of the time. Bodily fluids were everywhere. But there were moments of grace. I hadn't showered and only received one sponge bath during my four weeks in the hospital. I could not put on those grippy hospital socks myself and would often walk across the room barefoot. Consequently, my feet were exceptionally gross, and I was fairly certain I would end up with athlete's foot on top of everything else (I did).

During one evening visit my husband offered to wash my feet for me. In the church we wash people's feet on Maundy Thursday because Jesus washed his disciples' feet, but most people make sure their feet are extra clean. To have someone, even my husband, wash my filthy and infected feet felt intimate and holy. I found myself weeping uncontrollably, and, in that moment, I saw angels dancing in the windows. It sounds so trite that I am embarrassed to admit it. But it's true. I had a vision of angels dancing. I don't know that our prayers will heal you, but I hope that they will help you feel a connection to something holy and maybe even see the angels I saw. And if that doesn't work, I hope you will laugh a little. There is some crazy shit that happens when you are in the hospital. Stephen Colbert likes to say, "You cannot laugh and be afraid at the same time." Fear was my most constant companion when I was in the hospital, except for those rare moments of grace and laughter. I pray that some of these prayers will bring you laughter, and if that doesn't work, ask someone to demonstrate how a purewick works. If you can get a male nurse, even better.

PRAYING MY SURGEON
ISN'T HUNG OVER

> While in their joy they were disbelieving and still won-
> dering, he said to them, "Have you anything here to eat?"
> They gave him a piece of broiled fish, and he took it and
> ate in their presence.
>
> —LUKE 24:41-43

Jesus, who ate with your disciples even after resurrection:
I am about to undergo major surgery, putting my life into your
hands and the hands of another human. Please guide *their*
hands, Jesus. I pray that *they* are not hung over or craving a
food that will make *them* rush the surgery. That *they* didn't
have a big fight with their partner or child this morning. That
they are not distracted. That *they* aren't feeling a tickle in their
throat that will lead to *them* breathing or coughing infection
into an open wound in my body, even though I know that's
why *they* wear a surgical mask. Help *them* keep a firm grasp
on all their instruments so that they don't leave anything behind in my body. Please, Jesus, focus *them* on cutting out the
contagion. Amen.

PRAYER BEFORE
HIGH-RISK SURGERY

Jesus the Healer, help me feel content with all I have accomplished and with all the love in my life. Help me hold in my heart the dreams I have for what is to come so that I may push through the post-op challenges. Show the surgeon that I am a person instead of a collection of organs. When I awake, let me sense your presence. Amen.

PRAYER FOR
DIAPER DELIVERANCE

Dear God, who occasionally told people to don sackcloth, I would gladly take sackcloth over this diaper. I am both too young and too old to be wearing a diaper. Here I am, lying in a diaper because there is too much liquid flowing through me. Deliver me from the diaper. I long for real underwear. Being changed like an infant—there is nothing so demoralizing. Please, God, make this all go away. Give me control over my body so I can return to a life without diapers and catheters. Is this my sackcloth? Am I atoning for something? Can it be over now? Deliver me from the diaper. Amen.

PRAYER OF LONGING
FOR UNDERWEAR

> Thus said the Lord to me, "Go and buy yourself a linen loincloth, and put it on your loins, but do not dip it in water."
>
> —JEREMIAH 13:1

God, I know you care about underwear because you told Jeremiah to buy some and get them good and dirty to make a point about the pride of Judah. I am tired of being in the hospital without underwear. Please, Lord, let me get home and put on some damn panties. Clean ones. Amen.

IN PRAISE
OF HOSPITAL UNDERWEAR

Dear God, thank you for this amazing underwear. When they said that one size fits all, I didn't believe it because that is never true. But I think this underwear is miraculous because it fits me perfectly, and it's so comfy and stretchy. Thank you for underwear that stretches to fit my swollen body because, really, who wants tight underwear when you are sick and in pain? God, I know I shouldn't say this, but putting on this underwear made me believe a little more. Amen.

PRAYER BEFORE
A HOSPITAL MEAL

But he answered, "It is written,
'One does not live by bread alone,
but by every word that comes from the mouth
of God.'"

—MATTHEW 4:4

Dear God, who told us that we could not live on bread alone, I need you to know that I cannot drink one more Ensure. I know it's good for me and it has all kinds of awesome protein that will help me heal, but it tastes like death. So much tastes like death here. Please share some manna from heaven, but hold the quails. Amen.

PLEA AGAINST VOMITING

Dear God, don't let me throw up again. I am not asking that I enjoy the meal. This is hospital food, and one can only ask so much. I am weary of throwing up. The smell loiters like an unwelcome guest. Nothing can get rid of it. Let this food provide me with the nourishment I need to heal. Thank you for nourishment. I know I should be thankful to have any food at all. Just let it stay in my stomach. And, God, it would be really awesome if I could get the real ice cream this time. Amen.

CONSTIPATION PRAYER

Dear God, no one likes to talk about this, but it's real. Constipation makes every illness worse. Sometimes painkillers cause it. Sometimes the hospital food. And then when you finally go, you have to show the nurse the poop, because things aren't humiliating enough in the hospital. Nothing is private. God, please help me with my pride. May I release it. This is my body. This is what it is supposed to do. I will not be ashamed of what my body is supposed to do. I promise I will let go of my pride if you will help me let go of my poop. Please, God, get it out of me. If I have to eat any more applesauce laced with Metamucil, I may just have to resign myself to constipation. Amen.

PRAYER BEFORE GOING
TO THE BATHROOM

Dear God, I have to get up and walk to the bathroom, in these socks with the funny grippers on the bottom. It's so hard to go to the bathroom. There is equipment I have to drag and heart monitors that alert hospital staff when my heart rate soars. I am out of breath as I walk the short distance, and that shames me. Give me strength, God. I am supposed to carry your cross, and I can't even walk six feet without taking a break. I hate being this weak. If you can't give me strength, at least let me reach for you in my weakness. But mostly, let me reach the toilet before I pass out. Amen.

PRAYER AFTER HEART HARM

Jesus, your body held a heart like mine: one that beat and stopped beating. Did your heart begin beating again before you took a breath in the tomb? Your sacred heart is sometimes shown flaming, and I have felt like my heart was on fire, but yours is used for devotion while my hot heart made me think I was dying. Imagining your heartbeat comforts me as my own heart heals, as I painstakingly increase gentle exercise so that I can function in the world again. Strengthen my heart, Jesus. Amen.

PRAYER FOR THE ALARM THAT
WON'T STOP GOING OFF

Sleep is elusive here, God, with people constantly coming in to take my blood pressure or with a portable x-ray machine or more medicine. They are doing their jobs. But, sweet Jesus, I need you to silence that random alarm that won't stop going off. Clearly nothing is actually alarming because the noise never leads anyone to come in here until I press the call button to ask them to turn it off, please. Assuage my guilt for constantly pushing the call button about this. Amen.

PRAYER FOR GOD'S PRESENCE

Dear Jesus, who promised to send the Holy Spirit when you left this earth, where are you? I am lonely. How can a place with so many people coming and going through all hours of the night be so damn lonely? I used to talk to you all the time, Jesus. Now I am desperate for your presence. I want to feel you next to me, instead of these horrible hospital pillows that smell like wheat for reasons I cannot fathom. I hate all smells associated with the hospital. Would that I could smell you, Holy Spirit. I now understand why people use incense, because right now I want to sense you, and since I cannot hear you or see you, I would be okay with smelling you. I bet you smell like lavender. Amen.

PRAYER ABOUT MISSING
YOUR PET IN THE HOSPITAL

God, you brought forth all the creatures of the earth, but my pet (*name*) does not know why I am away. Let those who care for my pet show extra love. Give my pet rest and peace and grant us a joyful reunion soon. Amen.

A CURSE AGAINST TYLENOL

God, please curse the distributors of Tylenol. I know cursing is wrong, but the psalmists do it, and I thought I would at least ask. Why must the nurse wake me in the middle of the night for Tylenol? If all I needed was Tylenol, I would not be in the hospital. Curse them and their deal with the hospital to push it on patients and interrupt my precious sleep. And if I can't curse big pharma, give me a way to kindly tell them I don't want their damn Tylenol. Amen.

PRAYER FOR AN ADVOCATE

Dear Holy Spirit, Jesus left you with his disciples as an advocate. Right now, I need an advocate in human form. I love you, God, but I am not sure anyone in the hospital is listening to you. I am confused and afraid, and no one seems to have answers. No one has time and all I have is time, to wait and wonder if I will ever be better again. If you cannot send me someone in the flesh, please stay with me and slow my heart rate and my breathing so I do not fear the terror or the night. Give me some peace that doesn't come in a pill or a syringe. Amen.

PRAYER BEFORE CHEMOTHERAPY

> He has filled me with bitterness,
> he has sated me with wormwood.

–LAMENTATIONS 3:15

Lord, in Lamentations you sated with wormwood. Help my body welcome the medicine today that feels like poison. Help me focus on the warm blanket over my legs instead of this cold room; lemon cookies instead of the metal taste inside my mouth; tender nurses instead of the blue coats they don before they hook me up to these toxic bags. Crush this cancer under my foot. Amen.

5

WELL-WISHERS
AND CAREGIVERS

Years ago, I (Elizabeth) had a thirty-two-year-old parishioner with brain cancer. I officiated at his wedding and baptized his daughter just prior to the surgery that would give him a chance. He was overcome by the ways people were caring for him and his family during their ordeal.

"It's too bad it took something like this to make me grateful," he said, then showed me his arm, spotted from IVs. "I look like a heroin addict."

"No," I told him. "No." I searched for something more to say. Something true. "Because you don't have those bad teeth."

"That's meth," he said. "The bad teeth are meth addicts."

I tried again. "People would see the scars on your head and their first thought wouldn't be 'oh, a heroin addict,'" I said, then was immediately horrified that I had drawn attention to his surgical scars when attempting comfort.

But he lit up. "Do you know what I'm going to do? When I get out of here, I am going to shave my head so I see those scars every day in the mirror. Every single day. So I will always remember this, all that people have done for me. Does that make sense?"

He died two months later. I have thought about him and that conversation often over the years, and even more since getting cancer myself. His words make more sense than ever. I have a seven-inch scar on my back that no one sees—not even me, unless I put on my glasses, lift up my shirt, and twist in the bathroom mirror. I long for a reminder "every single day" of all that people have done for me. Thinking about how much my spouse has done and continues to do makes me especially emotional, as does thinking about nurses and doctors who have cared for me. I also know from people I've met in various support groups that not everyone experiences outpourings of support.

The first time I contracted cancer, my friend Sean—also a pastor—said to me, "You have to give your congregation something to do for you." So I told them to send cards but not casseroles, because I envisioned cheesy sausage casseroles jammed uneaten into our freezer and having to keep track of (and maybe accidentally breaking) faded green or brown dishes that weren't ours. But many of my clergy friends and nonchurch friends who had not received that message brought meals, bread, and cookies. Some were homemade, some purchased, some sent through DoorDash. With my second cancer, when people asked what they could do, I replied "send candy" until I had candy coming out of every crevice in my writing room (named the Samantha Suite after my friend and cowriter), including so many gummy bears that we took some to the children next door. With my relapse, every time I open the refrigerator or freezer and see quiches and soup feels like opening a love letter.

It can be harder to admit that I need those meals than to seek help from a medical professional. After all, I pay them (or at least my insurance company does). Still, I struggle with relying on physicians and nurses, as did Samantha, so we have included some prayers about these struggles in this section, as well as prayers about the people closest to us who have offered their care. We now add feelings of indebtedness to our love for them.

At the risk of committing a sin per the Book of Common Prayer's Litany of Penitence, where on page 268 one repents "for all false judgments, for uncharitable thoughts toward our neighbors, and for our prejudice and contempt for those who differ from us," sometimes gifts from well-wishers baffle me. Like mastectomy paper dolls, or lilies when I am allergic, or fake flowers and plants after they learned I was allergic to lilies. Piles of knit hats for my supposedly bald head in the hot humid summer when I was on chemo but did not lose my hair. So many lotions that I did not have to buy any for three years (some led to rashes). Orchids or other living plants that I killed from neglect, making me feel guilty. Books, some of which delighted me, and others I would never read but felt I shouldn't donate because they were a gift. Both Samantha and I received many, many blank journals—so many we planned to regift the surplus at a writing and yoga retreat we intended to lead but that kept getting called off due to our illnesses.

My parishioners took me at my word about cards instead of casseroles and sent literal stacks of cards instead. After my relapse, they set up a station at church where people could select and write cards, and my husband would gather and bring them to me on Sundays after service. Sometimes Dana, a member of my staff who took my dog to the church on Thursdays like I used to, would bring cards to me when dropping Pepper back home. Some cards included complaints about how things were going in my absence, which made wishes of "Get well soon" suspect. Did they want me to hurry up and get well so I could address their complaints? Sometimes I felt like cards downplayed the severity of what was happening with me. I often felt the cards pressured me to a positivity I did not feel. Then I received my favorite card, handmade from a six-year-old girl: "HOP YOU SRVIV." "That's what we're all thinking," the child's mom said to me later when I told her how much the card delighted me, "but the rest of us didn't have the nerve to say it."

Some gifts and expressions from well-wishers frustrate us, such as when people tell us what doctors we should consult or that raw honey cures cancer or that we should eat five pounds of blueberries a week or that a vegan diet will work better than radiation and chemotherapy, but we hesitated writing prayers reflecting that because we are also deeply grateful for all of it, especially the tender care from our spouses and family members. I understand that young man's desire to walk around with his scar showing to remember all that people had done for him. I want to shout my thanks and I pray about it often, and I wonder whether such gratitude belongs in a book with "irreverent" in its title.

Even when people say something we experience as problematic, they mean well, and a comment we don't like could have had great meaning to and comfort for someone else. We further recognize that our positions as pastors mean we have an unusually large pool of well-wishers while many (most?) who battle illness do not. Any perceived criticism can sound catty, ungrateful, and even unchristian. But our aspiration here is to be as authentic as we can about what we went through and continue to combat. So we offer these prayers with both ambivalence and trepidation as well as love and humor. While some words or gifts might initially sting, they tend to make us laugh later when we text each other.

GET WELL SOON

Dear God, the Creator of the world, I will not get well soon. Can you please tell my wonderful friends and family to stop telling me that they are praying for a "speedy recovery"? It makes me feel like there is a timeline and I am not adhering to it. If I could get better faster, I would. I know that you created all the world and all that is in it in seven days. Perhaps that has messed with people's expectations of a reasonable recovery. It might be time to remind people that Paul said Jesus was coming right back, and that was over two thousand years ago. Some things take a little longer than seven days. And, God, could you put in a word with the greeting card industry? Smite the words "speedy" and "quick." Amen.

PRAYER FOR PATIENCE FOR THE PEOPLE WISHING ME A SPEEDY RECOVERY

God, everyone wants me to get well fast, or at least that's what they say in their messages and texts, emails and cards. Their well-meaning wishes fuel my anxiety. Slow them down, God. Give them realistic expectations. Help me to be less annoyed with them because they mean well and this whole thing is going to take a long, long time. Amen.

IN THANKSGIVING FOR THE GIFT OF A PLANT THAT I AM SUPPOSED TO KEEP ALIVE DURING TREATMENT

Gracious God, giver of all good gifts: help me to not kill this plant that someone gave me. Help it to create more oxygen in my home. And if it does die, let me compost it without guilt. Help me to feel grateful that someone loves me and gave me something alive to care for. In the name of the one who gave his life so that I may live. Amen.

PRAYER FOR WELL-MEANING
FRIENDS AND FAMILY

> And Peter took him aside and began to rebuke him, saying,
> "God forbid it, Lord! This must never happen to you."
>
> —MATTHEW 16:22

Dear Jesus, whose devoted disciples occasionally said the wrong thing, did you notice that often your closest disciples said the exact wrong thing when you talked to them about your suffering? They didn't want you to suffer, so they argued with you or changed the subject. My friends and family love me, and they don't want me to suffer. They tell me to "get better fast" and "enjoy my time at home." It feels like pressure or complete ignorance. I can't control how fast I get better or even if I get better. And knowing people have a schedule in mind makes me feel like I am disappointing them. I know they mean well, but I don't want promises of subtle demands. I want them to say, "This is horrible and you don't deserve this." Amen.

PRAYER TO ANSWER
"HOW ARE YOU?" HONESTLY

Holy Spirit, send me the strength to answer "how are you?" honestly instead of feeling the need to comfort the questioner. Open my ears to hear that question as an invitation to be honest about my terror and depression over this situation. Please also make my questioners' tongues heavy so that they don't try to make me feel better but instead just hear me. Also, open my eyes so that I see their needs as well, and help me to ask and honestly care about how they are right now. Amen.

PRAYER FOR JOEL OSTEEN'S
KIND OF BLESSINGS

> Then he looked up at his disciples and said:
> "Blessed are you who are poor,
>> for yours is the kingdom of God.
> Blessed are you who are hungry now,
>> for you will be filled.
> Blessed are you who weep now,
>> for you will laugh."

—LUKE 6:20-21

Dear Jesus, who preached the double-edged blessings, tell the people who keep telling me how lucky I am to stop saying it. I know it. My doctors know it. My family knows it. But sometimes (not all the time) I don't feel lucky or even fortunate, which is the word that I also hear. I feel blessed—you know, that double-edged blessing you promised at the Sermon on the Mount. The people who were blessed were always the people who were still suffering, so you gave them a blessing. What a bunch of crap. Please, Jesus, take this blessing from me. I don't want this kind of blessing. I want a Joel Osteen blessing—you know, the kind that doesn't require suffering. Amen.

PRAYER WHEN PEOPLE CALL ME BRAVE OR INSPIRING

Gracious God, help me to react graciously when well-meaning people call me brave. I'm not brave. I didn't choose this and wouldn't if I had a choice. All I do when I am not at treatment is sit around or sleep, which is hardly inspiring. I should pray that you shield them from knowing that they would react as they must if they were in this situation too, but I would like them not to say stupid things in the future. So, please sort it out, God. Amen.

PRAYER FOR MY TIRED SPOUSE

Dear Creator God, who rested on the seventh day, I know that my spouse is tired, and I feel bad for all *he* has to do. At the same time, I have a hard time being compassionate. I would give anything to be that kind of tired—the kind of tired that wakes up in the morning, goes to work, and does productive things. I would like to be overwhelmed with all that I am doing. Instead, I stare at the wall and wonder if my emotional state is as fragile as my body. I think it is. God, help me be more compassionate to those who are caring for me. I know they are weary and overburdened. I can't help them. I can't even have patience when they don't get what I need fast enough. But you can help them. I know you can. May their sleep be deep and may they find comfort in your presence with them. Help me be better at saying please. And, God, it pains me to ask this, but let me be a little more patient. Amen.

PRAYER OF THANKS
FOR MY ELDERLY PARENTS

Dear God the Father and Mother, my parents would not appreciate being called elderly, but they are. Yet they were the ones who visited me every day while I was in the hospital—despite it being the peak of COVID and them being . . . elderly. I felt so much guilt because I thought I was supposed to be taking care of them, but there they were bathing their middle-aged daughter. I am so damn lucky. No matter how depressed and scared I was, I never stopped being grateful for my parents. One day soon, I know I will be caring for them. May I have just a fraction of their selflessness and compassion. I want to be good like them, but mostly, I want them to live forever. Amen.

A PLEA FOR JESUS TO TALK
TO MY DOCTOR

Jesus, who healed people and spoke to them in words they could understand, can you please have a chat with the doctors who start talking at me as soon as they walk in the room and wake me out of a dead sleep? Please wake them in the middle of the night and tell them something really important and then leave before they can ask for clarification. Make sure they remember just enough to be frustrated by the message and unable to convey it to other people. Amen.

AN IRRITABLE PRAYER
FOR DOCTORS

I the LORD your God am a jealous God.

Dear God, who can be a little jealous sometimes, some of my doctors seem to think they are God. I felt you should know, as you are God and it might be in your best interest to correct them. I am just looking out for you, God. You're welcome. Amen.

ANOTHER PRAYER TO
A JEALOUS GOD

Lord who heals: sometimes I think my surgeon is you. Please help bring me back to reality, especially since you proclaimed that you are a jealous God. *He's* just a guy with a knife. Thank you, the one true God, for making *him* brilliant and using *him* to save my life. Amen.

Dear God, please tell medical professionals never to use the excuse "it's a mystery." I thought that was your thing. Isn't that copyright infringement? Amen.

THANKSGIVING FOR THE NURSE WHO WAS CALM ABOUT MY BLOOD

> But the angel said to them, "Do not be afraid; for see—I am bringing you good news of great joy for all the people."
>
> —LUKE 2:10

God, who sends angels to tell us not to be afraid: thank you for the nurse who calmly told me that my leaking wound looked worse than it was, and coolly spoke to me with a small smile as she moved me from the blood-soaked chair to the bed and stopped the blood before getting help to clean up the room that looked like a crime scene. Such placidity is not one of my gifts, and I needed an angel to tell me to buck up. Amen.

PRAYER WHEN THE WELL-WISHERS HAVE MOVED ON

The rabble among them had a strong craving, and the Israelites also wept again, and said, "If only we had meat to eat! We remember the fish we used to eat in Egypt for nothing, the cucumbers, the melons, the leeks, the onions, and the garlic; but now our strength is dried up, and there is nothing at all but this manna to look at." ... "Consecrate yourselves for tomorrow, and you shall eat meat; for you have wailed in the hearing of the LORD, saying, 'If only we had meat to eat! Surely it was better for us in Egypt.' Therefore the LORD will give you meat, and you shall eat. You shall eat not only one day, or two days, or five days, or ten days, or twenty days, but for a whole month—until it comes out of your nostrils and becomes loathsome to you—because you have rejected the LORD who is among you, and have wailed before him, saying, 'Why did we ever leave Egypt?'"

—NUMBERS 11:4–6, 18–20

God, who made the Israelites eat meat until it came out of their nostrils after they complained: weeks ago, I had piles of presents and food that I could not finish and my phone was constantly buzzing from queries about my health, but now all is still. Perhaps they believe that the crisis has passed and all is well, or maybe they just made a casserole and moved on. Forgive me for my prior snarkiness. The care I received was not loathsome. Please nudge someone to send a text. Amen.

PRAYER FOR THOSE WHO
DO NOT HAVE WELL-WISHERS

God, who sees all, the prayers in this section sometimes complain about people who care for the patient and wish him or her well. I am not surrounded by such people. I feel alone. Please send me some people to bring me casseroles and orchids or fake flowers, or to call me brave or inspiring. I promise to be more appreciative than those who pray those other prayers about well-wishers. Amen.

6

AFTERMATH

As someone who has struggled with anxiety most of my adult life, I (Samantha) have always found comfort in Luke 12:22-26. "He said to his disciples, 'Therefore I tell you, do not worry about your life, what you will eat, or about your body, what you will wear. For life is more than food, and the body more than clothing. . . . Consider the lilies, how they grow: they neither toil nor spin; yet I tell you, even Solomon in all his glory was not clothed like one of these.'" In anxious moments, I would remind myself, "Consider the lilies." Yet when that verse came to me as I was lying in my own urine and blood, I thought, "Seriously, Jesus? That's the best you got?"

I was diagnosed with general anxiety when I was in my midtwenties. My anxiety was never rooted in fear of death. I wasn't preoccupied by that fear like others I knew, but I was definitely more sensitive to "things that could possibly go wrong" than your average person. I learned through therapy that, when experiencing anxiety, I was to imagine myself telling a friend the story the next day, which enabled me to step outside of myself. While my fears and anxieties never went away, I found a way to coach myself out of them. I learned that I could not rely on my instincts. I took a step back and considered the lilies.

I was convinced that I had a pulled muscle. That was the most logical assumption, as I had been on a hike the day before. The pain was extraordinary—yet I convinced myself that I had a low pain threshold, and I would embarrass myself if I went to the doctor. By the time I could not walk, crawl, sleep, or eat, I really didn't care what others thought of me, so I went in my pajama pants, my hair drenched with sweat in the 30-degree weather. By then it was almost too late. I was in septic shock by the time I got to the emergency room. I, the person who went to urgent care when I had an ear infection or a stye in my eye, almost died because I convinced myself I was overreacting.

When I returned from the hospital the first time, I was determined never to go back. Two days after I got home, I had a fever and chills. I called two friends, who assured me I was probably having an anxiety attack. Fortunately, I called my sister-in-law, who is a nurse practitioner, and she told me to go to the emergency room immediately. I went, once again assuming I was being foolish and preparing myself to be told I was fine. I was in the hospital for two more weeks.

When I returned from the hospital for the second time, everyone rejoiced and congratulated me. I stared at the wall and wondered if I could ever return from this mentally. I thought, when they tell my story, they will say this was when she broke. Because now that all my anxieties and fears came true, I could no longer trust the rational part of my psyche. The irrational part was what would keep me alive. The rational part was what kept me from going to the hospital in the first place. Common sense had almost killed me. I also realized that I needed more than "consider the lilies." It wasn't working. In fact, it actually enraged me when I thought of that passage.

I was happy to be out of the hospital but terrified to be at home. The night was the most dreadful time. I scrolled through Facebook to see if there was anyone awake. I saw random people "active" on messenger and sent them messages at 2:00 a.m. They were all asleep. Stupid Facebook Messenger. I told myself if I could just make it to 5:00 a.m., I could text Elizabeth, as I knew she woke at 4:55 so she could start writing at 5:00 a.m. As the days and weeks went by, things got better. I was sleeping for more than two hours at a time. The further I got from the hospital, the safer I felt.

Yet even as I recovered in the safety of my home, the memories came back hourly. Anything could set me off. I had become sensitive to anything that smelled like the hospital, so I was always lighting candles, buying fragrant oils. My leg was not healing, and just looking at my wound led me to panic. I became convinced it would never heal. I had to return to the hospital for one more surgery. Part of me welcomed the surgery because the only time I ever felt free of anxiety was when I was anesthetized, but a bigger part of me feared I would be sucked in again and stuck there. Fortunately, I was there for only one night. In the end, I was lucky. My wound healed after six months, and I was able to return to most of my regular activities.

From my experience with a miscarriage ten years prior, I knew the anniversaries of trauma could be almost as painful as the trauma itself. That said, I didn't expect the absolute terror I felt on January 1, the one-year anniversary of the day my leg started to hurt. I became convinced that it would happen again. I clung to my husband at night, begging him not to make me go back to the hospital. Fortunately, I haven't had to return. Not yet.

I remember calling parishioners when they were released from the hospital and congratulating them because surely the worst was over, but now I know that the release from the hospital is only the beginning of recovery. The surgeries and antibiotics saved my life, but the healing didn't start until I came home. While I won't say that was the hardest part, it was scarier somehow. I had the presence of mind to be scared and didn't have a nurse to call when I became convinced I was having a heart attack. If I died in the night, no one would know.

If you have recently returned from the hospital, it's okay if you don't feel back to your normal self. It's normal to be scared all the time. Find a good therapist. Find a friend who has also had this experience. Pray these prayers. I hope they will keep you company when Facebook Messenger lies to you and tells you others are still awake. If, like me, you don't find comfort in the lilies, feel free to tell Jesus that. Tell Jesus exactly what you think of those lilies. You might just find that's the kind of prayer you need.

PRAYER FOR RELEASE

Dear God, I have been released from the hospital. I am healed. But I am not. Please release me from the anxiety that comes in the flashbacks and the regrets of what I could have done, should have done, better. Let me feel warm without panicking about a fever. Allow me to see a small cut on someone else's leg without my mind conjuring images of an infection. Forgive me my wallowing. Release me from memories that come in un-expected times and places and hinder my relationships. I want to be the me I was before the time in the hospital—but I know that will never be. Release me from the expectations. Let me find peace with the wounded person I have become. Amen.

PRAYER OF THANKS FOR
PHYSICAL THERAPISTS

Dear God, thank you for the physical therapists who pick up the pieces after the surgeries are over and the pain is still present. Give me the strength I need to complete the exercises that hurt the most but also make the most difference. May these therapists know that their compassion and persistence have helped my body and soul. They have given me grace that I could not give myself. Amen.

PRAYER FOR PROGRESS

Dear God, who moves slowly at times but always moves: thank you for progress—for walking without a limp and being able to move in ways my body had forgotten. Thank you for not letting me quit and reminding me that progress is slow . . . but still progress. May every step be a reminder of how fortunate I am to have these two legs. They may be imperfect, but they are your creation. Amen.

PRAYER FOR IVS AFTER CHEMO
AND LYMPH NODE REMOVAL

Savior of the world, whose blood is somehow in the wine drunk from Sunday silver chalices: please, please, please plump my tired veins so that the needle finds my blood swiftly. Steer the hands of the one who wields that syringe. Save me from the pain of multiple stabs and jabs. Amen.

PRAYER TO BE MORE GRATEFUL

Dear God, I am grateful to be alive. I am grateful to have two functioning legs. I know the odds were not in my favor. Yet while I may honor you with my lips, I am not there in my heart. Help me be truly grateful, because I am not quite there yet. Help me with my lack of gratitude. Amen.

PRAYER OF THANKS
FOR TYING MY SHOES

Dear Jesus, who only wore sandals. For so long I needed help putting my socks on and tying my shoelaces. It's too cold for sandals, and I need socks. But it was too painful to bend that far, and someone else had to finish getting me dressed every day. Not today. Today I put on both of my socks and tied my shoes. I am shamelessly proud of myself for this small victory. May I also remember to thank the person who has knelt by my impatient side and put my socks and shoes on. Amen.

PRAYER REQUESTING
FORGIVENESS FOR INGRATITUDE

Dear God, I remember when I was in the hospital bed and I looked down at my legs that couldn't move, I promised myself that if they were functional again, I would never complain about the fat and varicose veins—the imperfections of my body. I would embrace body positivity and celebrate all that my body could do instead of buying more and more shapewear to cover all that I hated. That lasted about a month. Please forgive me for taking my healthy body for granted so soon after my injuries. Forgive my superficiality and concern for how things look rather than how this incredible body you created can still move. Amen.

PRAYER ON RETURNING TO WORK

God, I don't know what to ask for. I don't want anyone to mention my absence or ask me about my illness. And yet, even though I don't want to talk about what has happened to me and where I have been and what it has done not only to my body but my spirit, I also don't want people to have the same expectations of me that they used to. Insulate them from my irrational wrath, God. Help me figure out how I want to be treated so that I can guide those with whom I work. Amen.

ODE TO MISSING ORGANS
(OR OTHER BODY PARTS)

"And even the hairs of your head are all counted."
–MATTHEW 10:30

O Lord, who does not make mistakes and counts the hairs on my head: you made me with certain body parts that now have chunks or whole pieces removed. Removing these diseased pieces supposedly meant granting me more days here in the world, but I miss those parts. I'm misshapen compared to the way you made me, and I can't function in the same way. Please make me feel better, God. Make the remaining bits burst with health. Give me a body that terrifies diseases that try to invade. Make chocolate better for my body than kale. Amen.

PRAYER WHEN FEELING
LIKE LAZARUS

> The dead man came out, his hands and feet bound with
> strips of cloth, and his face wrapped in a cloth. Jesus said
> to them, "Unbind him, and let him go."
>
> —JOHN 11:44

Jesus, who walked on earth and experienced our pain, joy, and temptations: grant me patience with those who seem shocked when they see me, like I'm Lazarus, stinking and stumbling around after days in a tomb. Provide me with patience for those who believe I am the same as I was before I got sick. Help me to remember how much you loved Lazarus. Let me see your joy as you watched your bound friend emerge from his grave. Loosen my resentments and annoyance so that I may greet everyone with peace and pour out love, that I might both receive and give grace. Amen.

PRAYER FOR MISSING
THE HOSPITAL

Dear Holy Spirit, I hate the hospital so much for so many reasons. So when I say this, know that I don't say this lightly. Take me back. Take me back to the hospital. I can't handle the fullness of life outside of the hospital. I can't handle being healed because that means I have to be strong again, and I've never been good at being strong. Take me back to that horrible bed and strung-out nurses. Take me back to the place where everything could be solved by an IV, a pill, or a surgery. And if you decide not to do that, Holy Spirit, make me whole. I lost a piece of myself when I was sick, the piece that believed that I was healthy and strong. Without it, I am trying to live my whole life with only part of me. I miss my ignorance. I don't want to know how incredibly fragile life is. I don't want to panic every time someone I love gets a fever because my fever meant I was near death. Heal me completely this time. If not, take me back. Amen.

PRAYER FOR VISITING A LOVED ONE IN THE SAME HOSPITAL WHERE I WAS A PATIENT

God, how could you have called me back to this place? Calm my quivering organs and soothe my bowels. Help me focus on the patient I came to see instead of myself. And make the whole thing go fast and bring the patient comfort. Amen.

PRAYER FOR THAT
RANDOM RUNNER

> Therefore, since we are surrounded by so great a cloud of
> witnesses, let us also lay aside every weight and the sin
> that clings so closely, and let us run with perseverance the
> race that is set before us.
>
> —HEBREWS 12:1

Jesus, forgive me for my fury at the random runner who panted
by me as I walked in the wind. It is not his fault that I can't run.
He has no idea what I have been through. Forgive me for not
returning his quick smile, for holding my breath as he ran past,
for sticking my face in my sweatshirt, for my wrath at him for
being on the wrong side of the road. Help his lungs drink in
clean air. Help me breathe in placidity. Amen.

PRAYER FOR ENERGY

> "Come to me, all you that are weary and are carrying heavy burdens, and I will give you rest."
>
> —MATTHEW 11:28

Jesus, who promised rest to the weary: I don't understand my lack of energy. My fatigue. Rest does not change anything. I need to be enlivened . . . maybe? Or maybe I just need more sleep. Maybe I need outdoor walks, time in the sun. But I'm exhausted and I just want rest, which makes me feel burdened with guilt. Everyone wants me to be better, and I feel too tired to want anything. Please, help. Amen.

PRAYER FOR MY CHILD

Dear Heavenly Father and Mother, please help my child through this difficult time. May *he* know that my inattention isn't a lack of love, it's a lack of health. I can't play. I can't even move from my bed. *He* wants the me who was here three months ago, and I want that me as well. Provide us both the patience that we need. Give me your grace that will allow me to accept myself as an absent parent for this period of my life. It will not always be this way, and *he* will survive this. We both will. Please help me hold my tears until *he* is out of the room. No child should see a parent cry this much. May *he* know that *he* is loved by his family and by you, God. Amen.

PRAYER TO FORGET

Dear God, I can't remember if I brushed my teeth this morning. But I remember exactly what I was wearing when I was wheeled into the ER that freezing night. My shoes were tight because my body was swollen. I remember the smell of the brown blankets that I sweat through the first few nights. I remember the shoes the nurse was wearing when she told me not to cry as I struggled to stand while sweat and blood drained down my legs. I remember the needles, the MRIs, the board they strapped me to during the endless test. I look at my long scar, and I can see the fear in the eyes of the doctor while he assured me that I would not lose my leg. I know how fear smells now, and I still smell it all the time.

Please help me forget the taste of the antibiotic that they drained into my body for months and the saline liquid that always felt cold going into my arms. When you showed your disciples your scars, was there a moment when the memories hit you and you too wanted to forget the agony, the sweat, and the betrayal? It seems like you remembered, but it didn't hurt you. How did that work? How did you heal in three days? It must be the whole divine thing. Since I am not divine, please just let me forget. Amen.

7

RELAPSE

"Preach from your scars, not your wounds," we both learned in preaching classes. Writers sometimes spout a similar maxim. But while working on this book, my lung cancer came back. First, I (Elizabeth) had gone from "NED"—no evidence of disease—to "stable," due to new nodules in what remained of my left lung. When people asked how I was and I replied, smiling, "stable," they looked at me as if I had violated some social contract. "You look so healthy," they would respond, which sounded to me like, "You've gained lots of weight and people with cancer are supposed to be skeletal and bald. So just say you're 'fine, thanks!'"

The nodules grew slowly over a year. Samantha was at my place working on this book with me when the surgeon called to say that he and his colleagues on an ominously named "Tumor Board" had determined I needed a PET scan. He indicated that could lead to more thoracic surgery: a "wedge," which meant removing a little slice from the remaining lobe of my left lung versus taking a whole lobe, as he had in April 2020.

Remembering the broken ribs, the breathlessness, the time in ICU, I felt devastated and was grateful that Samantha was with me writing prayers.

Just, please, let me keep what's left of my left lung, I prayed for weeks. I had read that when an entire lung is removed, the forlorn cavity fills with fluid. Sometimes I was sure I could feel my lung fragment moving around when I did yoga, but I was grateful that I still had something on that side.

When Gary and I met with the surgeon a month later to hear the PET scan results, we learned that multiple tumors had lit up, so a wedge wasn't possible. Only a pneumonectomy: entire removal of the lung. The surgeon wasn't sure he wanted to perform such an invasive surgery, as he was selective about who was healthy enough to achieve a good result. I had to undergo multiple breathing tests, some in a little glass booth and others attached to what looked like a scuba tank; a brain MRI while wearing a Hannibal Lecter-like mask; a "punch" biopsy, after which I had to lie still for an hour to make sure my lung didn't collapse. Though I was also told that if it did collapse that would just make it easier for the surgeon to remove.

My prayers changed from wanting to keep what was left of my left lung to pleading for the surgery. At the final meeting with the surgeon following all the tests, at which he would make a yes-or-no decision about the surgery, I carefully selected what to wear, texting choices to Samantha and our friend Andie. Glasses or not? Glasses make me look smarter, but without them I look younger, and we wanted to impress upon him that I was young enough to potentially have decades ahead of me if he would cut me open again. We decided

I would wear a clerical collar to remind him that I was an important and busy professional. I also brought a true crime library book with me to create a "give-me-a-surgery-date-or-I-will-murder-you-and-get-away-with-it" vibe. I don't know if the careful outfit and book selection helped, but he decided to move forward and scheduled a surgery date five days later.

This so-called recurrence of my cancer led me to abandon any pretense of writing from scars instead of wounds. I wanted to finish this book. In my own reading, I sought comfort not from writers who had been sick and then went on to thrive but from people who were still sick or died but left some words behind. This felt countercultural for a Christian, since we are quick to follow any mention of death with resurrection. But in the Old Testament, when David was at the end of his life, his followers hoped that a gorgeous young woman, Abishag the Shunamite, would help warm David up when he was old and couldn't get warm. (Didn't work. David died.)

As with my original bouts with cancer, the psalms brought me more comfort than anything else in the Bible. Psalm 6 became my favorite this time around, especially the second and third verses:

> Be gracious to me, O LORD, for I am languishing;
> O LORD, heal me, for my bones are shaking with
>   terror.
> My soul also is struck with terror,
> while you, O LORD—how long?

When the time came for surgery, I took the prayers Samantha and I had written so far with me into the hospital and was amazed by their breadth and accuracy in the hospital section: nausea, constipation, underwear. Samantha made me a laminated sign that read "STOP! Do not wake this patient up for Tylenol. She doesn't want the Tylenol. Seriously, don't wake her for Tylenol. God is watching." I was grateful to learn from the night nurses that they would not wake me up at midnight for Tylenol if I declined it in advance, and I hoped that this book could end up helping more people than just me who weren't interested in being awakened for a midnight dose of an over-the-counter analgesic.

Unfortunately, I also learned that part of one tumor remained after my lung was removed, on my aorta; and that three lymph nodes contained cancer. At the time I'm writing this, I'm scheduled for radiation and targeted therapy. I don't know how much longer I have to live. Over the past three years, I've screwed up the nerve three times to ask one of my doctors if he thinks I will still be alive in five years. He has twice said, without blinking, *yes*. But with this latest wrinkle, he responded, "I hope so." He also emphasized (after my eyes filled up) that the chances were *not* zero. I appreciate his honesty. I hope I will live for years and years, and that during that time thousands of people will pray some of these prayers. I hope some will pray these words after I'm gone, too.

PRAYER AFTER RECURRENCE

For he does not willingly afflict or grieve anyone.

—LAMENTATIONS 3:33

God, who does not willingly afflict anyone: help me to feel grateful that it's different this time, that when meeting with the physician polysyllabic medical terms flow off my tongue. Diffuse my anger at having to suppress my feelings to comfort other people. Help my loved ones to find the assurance they seek and can only find in you. Open my eyes to the work of the Spirit in the midst of this. In the name of Jesus, who once healed with mud and spit. Amen.

PRAYER OF FORGIVENESS WHEN MY DOCTOR TURNS OUT NOT TO BE GOD

God, who insists on being the only god: I thought my surgeon was going to be able to fix this, but he can't. Neither can my other doctors. Help me to forgive them for not being you. Forgive me for wanting them to be all-powerful miracle workers. Help me place all of my trust in you, the one god, the only one, the only God. Amen.

AN ANGRY RECURRENCE PRAYER

> Be angry but do not sin; do not let the sun go down on your
> anger, and do not make room for the devil.
>
> —EPHESIANS 4:26-27

Jesus, it is night. The sun has gone down. The sun has gone down, and I am still angry that this cancer has come back. Does that mean I've made room for the devil? Is he having a party in my body alongside the tumors? I pray that the devil and the tumors will choke each other and be forever expunged from my body. I pray that they will drown like the pursuing Egyptians were drowned as they chased their former slaves through the parted Red Sea. I pray that they will be consumed by a lake of fire. Amen.

PRAYER OF DARKNESS

Even the darkness is not dark to you;
   the night is as bright as the day,
   for darkness is as light to you.

—PSALM 139:12

Oh God, for whom the night is as bright as the day: since my most recent bad news I have trouble doing anything, including praying to you. Let me be lifted on the prayers of others. Help me to see life and eternity through your eyes. Help me not to dwell on what is not yet done, on what I have not done, on what I will never do. Let darkness comfort me, so that I do not discriminate between dark and light. Amen.

PRAYER FOR SELFISHNESS

Gracious God, I feel like I have to protect others from my bad news. I try not to disclose too much, or to make my illness funny or be lighthearted about it, or to keep it from them altogether. Please, God, strengthen them so that I don't have to try to shield them from my reality. Steel them so that they can handle hearing what I'm having to live with: fury, pain, struggle. Let me be pissed off, pensive, petrified. Let me be a little selfish for a little while. Amen.

PRAYER FOR OTHERS
DURING RELAPSE

> You shall not take vengeance or bear a grudge against any
> of your people, but you shall love your neighbor as your-
> self: I am the LORD.

—LEVITICUS 19:18

God, who commands us to love our neighbors as ourselves:
I rarely care about anything beyond myself anymore. My
world has constricted, and loved ones try to expand it a little
by telling me about their lives, but I have to force myself to act
curious and ask questions. I can't even listen to the news or
finish a Netflix series or a book. I'm sad in the morning when I
wake from dreams in which I was well. Maybe I can't care because I'm mad imagining a world without me in it. Please, God:
help me to love my neighbors as much as I used to. Amen.

PRAYER ABOUT HOPE

> And not only that but we also boast in our sufferings,
> knowing that suffering produces endurance, and endur-
> ance produces character, and character produces hope,
> and hope does not disappoint us, because God's love has
> been poured into our hearts through the Holy Spirit that
> has been given to us.
>
> —ROMANS 5:3–5

Holy Spirit that God's love poured into my heart: I can't boast
of my sufferings because that would annoy people. Forgive
me for the way I used to get bored when old people discussed
their various pains in detail. Forgive me for being angry with
the words I used to love about suffering, endurance, character, and hope. Forgive me for the fury that chokes my throat
whenever someone speaks about hope. I know I must find
some hope. If you can't fill me with hope, please help me find
a flutter of it. Amen.

RADIATION REDUX

> There the angel of the LORD appeared to him in a flame of fire out of a bush; he looked, and the bush was blazing, yet it was not consumed.
>
> –EXODUS 3:2

God, who can burn bushes while leaving them intact: let these radiation beams burn up the tumors without incinerating my surrounding organs and bones. Give me the patience of Moses as he turned aside to see the blazing bush as I go, day after day, to don a dingy wrinkled robe and lie with my arms over my head on a plank of a massive white machine while techs move my body to line up tiny tattoos with an invisible guide. Support me through the days and weeks to the other side. Amen.

PRAYER WHEN FEELING GUILT FOR INSUFFICIENT APPRECIATION OF A GORGEOUS DAY

God, who created everything that exists: today's beautiful in an unseasonable way. I should go outside to appreciate your handiwork in the world, but all I want to do is sit in this chair or sleep. I don't know whether to pray that you enliven me to get up and go out there or soothe me so that I may rest without reproach. I trust you to choose. Amen.

PRAYER FOR A GRIM PROGNOSIS

> They have treated the wound of my people carelessly,
>> saying, "Peace, peace,"
>> when there is no peace.
>
> —JEREMIAH 6:14

God, the stats look bad for me, at least if I want to stick around here. I am sick of people seeing me as an inspiration. I don't want to die yet. I know you understand because of the Jeremiah quote, "'Peace, peace,' when there is no peace." I don't want peace, God. I want to live. Channeling Augustine, whom you love even though I find him irritating: bring me peace, but not yet. Amen.

PRAYER AFTER LOSING LONGEVITY

He has shortened my days.

—PSALM 102:23B

God, with this sickness my days have been shortened. Help me to embrace the life that I have left. Guide me to choose the things that will leave the biggest impact. Help me to see the life lurking everywhere: the shoots creeping up in winter, the buds on bushes and trees. Show me beauty in stark cold and dark. Narrow my focus to that which matters most. In the name of all that is holy. Amen.

PRAYER ABOUT GRATITUDE

Then Jesus asked, "Were not ten made clean? But the other nine, where are they? Was none of them found to return and give praise to God except this foreigner?"

—LUKE 17:17–18

Jesus, who criticized nine men he healed that did not thank him: I am trying to be grateful despite my illness. I ache from my surgery but know that surgery is not an option for all. I am weary from treatments, but I know that some receive no treatments at all. Being this sick has helped me prioritize what's most important, so I am at least a little appreciative. People live in countries where treatments aren't available. People live in this country without health insurance, and I have health insurance. Please help me to feel truly thankful, because I am fortunate even though I can't be cured. Help me remember that we are all dying anyway. Help me not feel singled out, yet to be the one who turns back to thank you. Amen.

PRAYER WHEN CONTEMPLATING QUITTING ONE'S JOB DUE TO MEDICAL ISSUES

How long shall this wicked congregation complain against me? I have heard the complaints of the Israelites, which they complain against me.

—NUMBERS 14:27

For surely I know the plans I have for you, says the LORD, plans for your welfare and not for harm, to give you a future with hope.

—JEREMIAH 29:11

Then he said to them all, "If any want to become my followers, let them deny themselves and take up their cross daily and follow me."

—LUKE 9:23

God, who did not give up on the Israelites even though they complained incessantly in the wilderness: I love my job but don't think I can do it anymore without wrecking my health. Is doing something that may be harming me a way of taking up a cross daily? I believe the promises you made through Jeremiah, wanting me to live a future with hope, but I do not know whether continuing to work at this vocation is an act of hope or barreling toward harm. I also don't know how I am supposed to scrape by financially without it. Please guide me. Amen.

PRAYER ABOUT HOW KIND EVERYONE IS WHEN THEY THINK YOU'RE DYING

He delivered me, because he delighted in me.

—PSALM 18:19

God, sometimes I forget that you delight in me because this is happening to me again, but then I see how people treat me right now and I remember. Everyone wants to help and be kind. There's a chance that I can beat this again: a small chance, but there. If I do, will people still be as sweet to me as they are right now when they think I am dying? I pray for a miracle, and that they will still be as sweet. Maybe half as sweet. I want to live. Amen.

PRAYER NOT TO BE BEATIFIED

God, who welcomes us into heaven: I have seen throughout my life that people who die when young or middle-aged become saintly in the memories of those they loved and left behind. Please, God who remembers, help my memory be a blessing to my beloveds when I am gone, but help them lovingly remember my flaws. How I don't detect dust or pet hair in my home but relish reality television and always crave candy. I don't mind if they forget the ways I wounded and failed them, but don't let them perfect me in their minds when I'm gone. Also, let me live longer than expected. Please. Amen.

ACKNOWLEDGMENTS

FROM SAMANTHA

I am grateful to my son Joshua for motivating me to get better so that I could keep up with him. I have forgiven him for eating chocolate at 9 p.m. while I lay in bed unable to stop him. I am beyond grateful to my husband, Conor, who did most of the heavy lifting while I was ill. He had help from his parents, who drove twelve hours to be with us. My parents visited me every day in the hospital, whatever hours they were allowed in. All three of my brothers also visited from other parts of the country and played with my son and made me laugh. Thanks to those who visited, especially: Andie Rohrs, Genevieve Nelson, Elise Myers, Bishop Susan Haynes, Lynn Farlin, and Lori Bergmooser. Thank you also to all those who brought me food, especially the good people of St. John's Episcopal Church.

Thanks to my orthopedic surgeon, Dr. Balsamo, and all the doctors who were involved in my care. There were also many nurses who worked so very hard, despite being tired and overworked. They deserve all of our gratitude. The home health-care workers, especially those who did physical therapy and wound care, were amazing.

There were many flowers and cards, and the flowers were what made the month in the hospital bearable. Many of them were from my church family, and I felt truly loved. I missed three months of work, but our associate rector, the Reverend Mark Riley, took care of the church while I was gone and ensured that I didn't have to worry.

To Elizabeth, you have always been the person I could open my heart to, but even more during this ordeal. Without you, this book would not have happened. It would have been an idea floating in my head. You made it a reality. You are a woman of valor.

FROM ELIZABETH

Having my lung cancer return in the midst of working on this book meant a lot of work for the people closest to me. Thanks especially to Gary, and to all those who visited us from Arizona and did all in their power to make our lives easier: Wendy Marshall; David Marshall; Betty Hancock; Jenny, Ryan, Alice, and Will Drzewiecki. Thanks to all who brought us food, especially Andie Rohrs; Gini DiStanislao; Dale Custer; Shea Tuttle; Travis Kennedy; Rita DeRosa; Jeunée Godsey; Nancy Meck. Deep thanks to Judie Belka, who came for my breast cancer surgery back before everything shut down.

Thanks to St. David's Episcopal Church, especially staff members Dana Blackman and Connie Sylvester and wardens Marti Stephens-Hartka and Hanby Carter. Thanks to the supply clergy who led worship in my absence: Andie Rohrs, Mario Gonzalez del Solar, Martha Jenkins, Ruth Partlow, and Barbara Marques.

Thanks to the physicians and nurses who cared for me, especially radiation oncologist David Randolph Sr., who made me a wooden cross that now faces me in my writing room (a.k.a. "the Samantha Suite").

Thanks to Dana VanderLugt, who reads what I write when it's rough, and to my clergy cowriting group Teri Ott, Melissa Earley, Celeste Kennel-Shank, Heidi Haverkamp, and Meghan Murphy-Gill.

I could fill a book with the names of people who cared for me when I was sick and supported me while writing this book.

Finally: thank you, Samantha. Thank you first for calling me from the ICU, and then for thinking of this book two months later. Thank you for the Tylenol sign, for the personal video message from my favorite Bravolebrity Meredith Marks (and Andy Cohen and Brooks!), and for creating a yoga routine just for me that took into account all that I can no longer do. I hate that we went through what we did but am grateful for our friendship and for creating these prayers with you.

FROM BOTH OF US

We are deeply grateful to Keely Boeving, our agent for this book; Sarah Gombis; and the team we worked with at Eerdmans: Lisa Ann Cockrel, Jason Pearson, Claire McColley, Caroline Jansen, Laurel Draper, William Hearn, James Ernest, Anita Eerdmans, Tom Raabe, Shane White, Jeff Dundas, and Kristine Nelson.